THE ULTIMATE PARENT'S GUIDEBOOK TO TEEN EXECUTIVE FUNCTIONING AND SOCIAL SKILLS

(2 Books in 1)

Fundamental Life Skills to Enhance Focus and Attention, Thrive in Social Settings, and Build Unstoppable Confidence

AMBER PRESTON

Table of Contents

Executive Functioning Skills for Teens
AMBER PRESTON

Social Skills for Teens
AMBER PRESTON

Executive Functioning Skills for Teens

A PARENT'S GUIDE TO EMPOWER TEENS TO IMPROVE FOCUS, GET ORGANIZED, SET PRIORITIES, AND GAIN FUNDAMENTAL LIFE SKILLS

Amber Preston

Introduction

It's a typical weeknight in the Johnson household. Fourteen-year-old Ethan is sprawled on the couch, his math textbook lying forgotten on the coffee table as he scrolls through his phone. His mother, Megan, stands in the doorway, a mixture of frustration and concern etched on her face.

"Ethan, have you started your homework yet?" she asks, already knowing the answer.

Ethan barely looks up. "I'll do it later, Mom. I've got time."

Megan sighs, remembering the unfinished project that's due tomorrow—the one Ethan swore he'd start days ago. She thinks about his backpack, a jumbled mess of crumpled papers and half-eaten snacks. And she can't help but worry about his grades, which have been slipping despite his obvious intelligence.

If this scene feels all too familiar, you're not alone. Countless parents find themselves in Megan's shoes, watching helplessly as their bright, capable teens struggle to manage their time, stay organized, and reach their full potential. It's a frustrating, often heartbreaking experience that leaves many parents wondering: Why can't my teen just get it together?

The answer lies in a set of crucial cognitive skills known as executive functions. These are the mental processes that enable us to plan, focus attention, remember instructions, and juggle multiple tasks successfully. They're the backbone of effective learning and productivity—and for many teens, they don't come naturally.

That's where this book comes in. It is your roadmap to understanding and nurturing these vital abilities in your teen. Whether your child is struggling with focus and organization or you simply want to give them a head start in life, this book offers the insights and strategies you need to make a real difference.

Why focus on executive functioning skills? Because they're the key to unlocking your teen's potential, both in school and in life. Cortés Pascual et al. (2019), research shows that strong executive functions correlate with:

- Better academic performance
- Higher self-control
- Improved mental health
- Greater success in future careers

In today's fast-paced, distraction-filled world, these skills are more crucial than ever. Teens face a constant barrage of notifications, social media updates, and information overload. Without strong executive functions, it's all too easy to get lost in the noise and lose sight of what's truly important.

But here's the good news: Executive functioning skills can be developed and strengthened with the right support and strategies. And as a parent, you're in the perfect position to provide that support.

This book is designed to empower you with the knowledge and tools you need to guide your teen towards greater focus, organization, and self-management. Here's what you can expect:

- Clear, jargon-free explanations of what executive functioning skills are and why they matter
- Practical, easy-to-implement strategies for boosting these skills in your teen
- Real-world case studies that bring the concepts to life
- Actionable exercises you can do with your teen to practice and reinforce new skills
- Tips for creating a home environment that supports executive function development
- Insights into how these skills impact academic performance, social relationships, and future success
- Guidance on when and how to seek professional help if needed

Each chapter focuses on a specific aspect of executive functioning, from time management and organization to emotional regulation and goal-setting. You'll find a mix of scientific insights, practical advice, and relatable anecdotes that make the information easy to understand and apply.

The strategies in this book are designed to be flexible and adaptable. Every teen is unique, and what works for one may not work for another. That's why there are a variety of approaches, allowing you to find the ones that resonate best with your child's personality and needs.

As you read, you'll notice that my goal is to be supportive, encouraging, and solution-oriented. I understand the challenges you're facing, and I'm here to offer hope and practical help—not judgment or unrealistic promises. I believe in progress over perfection, and I'll show you how to celebrate small wins along the way.

One of the most exciting aspects of working on executive functioning skills is that you can start seeing positive changes quickly. Many parents report noticeable improvements in their teen's behavior and performance within weeks of implementing these strategies. Of course, lasting change takes time and consistent effort, but those initial wins can be incredibly motivating for both you and your teen.

Before we start, a word of encouragement: By picking up this book, you've already taken a crucial step towards supporting your teen's success. Your commitment to understanding and nurturing their executive functioning skills will make a profound difference in their life—not just now, but for years to come.

So, are you ready to begin? To watch your teen grow in confidence, capability, and independence? To reduce family stress and create a more harmonious home environment? To set your child up for success in high school, college, and beyond?

Then let's get started. Turn the page, and take the first step towards empowering your teen with the executive functioning skills they need to thrive. Together, we'll transform those frustrating evenings into opportunities for growth, connection, and achievement.

Understanding Executive Functioning Skills

Your teen is sitting at the kitchen table, surrounded by open textbooks and half-finished assignments. They've been there for hours, but progress seems nonexistent. Sound familiar? What you're witnessing isn't laziness or a lack of intelligence—it's a struggle with executive functioning skills.

Executive functioning skills are the brain's air traffic control system. Just as air traffic controllers manage the flow of planes on runways and in the sky, these skills help us manage our thoughts, actions, and emotions. They're the mental processes that allow us to plan, focus attention, remember instructions, and juggle multiple tasks efficiently.

But what exactly are these skills? Let's break it down:

1. **Working memory:** This is the ability to hold and manipulate information in our minds. It's like a mental sticky note that helps us remember and work with information in the short term. For teens, this might mean keeping track of multiple steps in a math problem or remembering the key points they want to make in an essay.

2. **Flexible thinking:** This skill allows us to adapt to new situations and think about problems in different ways. It's about being able to shift gears when needed and consider alternative solutions. For example, a teen with good flexible thinking might easily pivot to a new study strategy if their usual method isn't working.

3. **Self-control:** Also known as inhibition, this is the ability to resist impulses and stay focused on tasks. It's what helps teens resist the urge to check their phone every five minutes while doing homework or avoid blurting out answers in class before being called on.

4. **Task initiation:** This is the skill of starting tasks promptly without undue procrastination. It's what gets a teen to open their textbook and start studying, even when they'd rather be doing something else.

5. **Organization and planning:** These skills involve structuring and managing tasks, information, or materials efficiently. This might look like a teen keeping their backpack organized, managing a calendar of assignments and activities, or breaking down a big project into manageable steps.

6. **Time management:** This is the skill of allocating and using time effectively to complete tasks. It's what helps a teen estimate how long an assignment will take, budget their time accordingly, and meet deadlines consistently.

7. **Emotional regulation:** This involves managing emotions to respond appropriately in different situations. It's the ability to stay calm under pressure, handle frustration without outbursts, and maintain a positive attitude in the face of challenges.

8. **Goal setting and prioritization:** These skills involve determining objectives and ranking tasks based on importance and urgency. It's what allows a teen to decide what homework to tackle first or how to balance studying with extracurricular activities.

These skills are distinct from general cognitive or academic abilities. While cognitive skills involve basic mental processes like memory and reasoning, executive functioning skills are about managing and coordinating these processes to achieve goals. It's the difference between knowing what steps to take and actually organizing those steps in a logical order and managing the time required for each.

Think of it this way: cognitive skills are like the individual musicians in an orchestra, each playing their instrument. Executive functioning skills are the conductor, coordinating all these individual elements to create a harmonious performance.

The development of executive functioning skills is a journey that starts in early childhood and continues well into adulthood. In the early years, children begin to develop basic self-control and simple planning abilities. As they enter middle childhood, more complex planning and organizational skills start to emerge. But it's during the teenage years that these skills really come into their own.

Adolescence is a critical period for the development of executive functioning. The teenage brain is undergoing significant changes, particularly in the prefrontal cortex—the area responsible for many executive functions. This period of neural plasticity presents both challenges and opportunities. On one hand, teens may struggle with impulse control and decision-making as their brains develop. On the other hand, this is a prime time for learning and strengthening these crucial skills.

Understanding this developmental trajectory is crucial for parents. It helps us set realistic expectations and provide appropriate support. We can't expect a 13-year-old to have the same level of organizational skills as an adult, but we can nurture the development of these skills in age-appropriate ways.

It's also important to recognize that executive functioning skills don't develop in isolation. They're heavily influenced by a child's environment and experiences. A supportive home environment, with consistent routines and opportunities for practice, can significantly enhance the development of these skills. Conversely, chaos, inconsistency, or lack of support can hinder their growth.

As parents, we play a crucial role in this process. By understanding these skills and actively supporting their development, we can help our teens build a strong foundation for success. In the chapters that follow, we'll explore specific strategies for nurturing each of these skills. But first, let's dive deeper into why these skills matter so much for our teens.

The Role of Executive Functioning in Teen Development

Now, let's consider how these skills impact your teen's daily life. Remember that homework struggle we mentioned earlier? Executive functioning skills are at the heart of it. When it comes to academics, these skills affect:

- Homework completion: Managing time, breaking down assignments, resisting procrastination. A teen with strong executive functioning skills can sit down after school, prioritize their assignments, break them into manageable chunks, and work through them efficiently without getting distracted.
- Studying for exams: Organizing materials, planning study sessions, maintaining focus. This might look like creating a study schedule, gathering all necessary materials, using effective study techniques, and staying focused during review sessions.
- Class participation: Remembering instructions, staying engaged, thinking flexibly. In class, these skills help teens follow along with lessons, contribute to discussions, and adapt to different teaching styles.

But it's not just about school. These skills are crucial for managing daily life and responsibilities. Think about your teen's packed schedule—school, extracurriculars, social commitments, chores. Strong executive functioning skills allow them to juggle these demands without feeling overwhelmed.

For instance, a teen with good time management and organization skills can balance soccer practice, a part-time job, and schoolwork without dropping the ball. They can plan their week, allocate time for each activity, and adjust their schedule as needed. They're less likely to forget about a shift at work or miss a homework deadline because they've developed systems to keep track of their responsibilities.

The benefits extend to social and emotional well-being too. Teens with strong executive functioning skills are better equipped to:

- Build and maintain relationships: They can remember plans with friends, show up on time, and manage conflicts more effectively.
- Handle social interactions: They're better able to read social cues, control impulses in social situations, and adapt their behavior to different social contexts.
- Manage stress: They can break down overwhelming tasks, prioritize self-care, and use strategies to calm themselves when feeling anxious.
- Navigate conflicts: They can think through problems logically, consider different perspectives, and come up with constructive solutions.

These skills contribute to greater emotional resilience. When faced with challenges, teens with strong executive functioning are more likely to approach problems calmly and systematically, rather than becoming overwhelmed or giving up.

On the flip side, weak executive functioning skills can have long-term consequences. They can impact:

- Career success: In the workplace, executive functioning skills are critical. Employees need to manage their time, meet deadlines, adapt to new challenges, and work effectively with others. Teens who struggle with these skills may find it harder to succeed in their chosen careers, potentially leading to job instability and dissatisfaction.
- Independence in adulthood: Many aspects of adult life rely heavily on executive functioning. Managing finances, maintaining a household, and navigating complex social landscapes all require these skills. Teens who haven't developed strong executive functioning may struggle to live independently, relying more on others for support.
- Overall well-being: Chronic difficulties with organization, time management, and emotional regulation can lead to increased stress, anxiety, and other mental health issues. Teens who struggle with these skills may experience lower self-esteem and less satisfaction with life overall.

It's important to note that executive functioning skills aren't fixed traits. They can be developed and strengthened over time with the right support and strategies. That's why understanding these skills is so crucial for parents. By recognizing their importance and actively nurturing them, we can set our teens up for success not just in school, but in all aspects of their lives.

In the next section, we'll explore some of the common challenges teens face when it comes to executive functioning. Understanding these challenges is the first step in helping our teens overcome them.

Common Challenges in Executive Functioning for Teens

If you're nodding along, recognizing your teen in these descriptions, you're not alone. Many teens struggle with executive functioning. Some common challenges include:

1. Procrastination: This is often the most visible sign of executive functioning difficulties. Teens might delay starting assignments until the night before they're due, or put off studying for tests until the last minute. This isn't just about being lazy—it often stems from difficulties with task initiation, time management, and breaking down large tasks into manageable steps.

2. Disorganization: You might notice this in your teen's messy backpack, cluttered desk, or lost assignments. Teens struggling with organization might have trouble keeping track of materials for different classes, managing their school papers, or maintaining a system for storing and retrieving information.

3. Poor time management: This shows up as difficulty estimating how long tasks will take, frequently running late, or struggling to balance multiple responsibilities. Teens might underestimate how long an assignment will take, leading to late nights and rushed work.

4. Difficulty with long-term projects: Projects that require planning and sustained effort over time can be particularly challenging. Teens might procrastinate starting, struggle to break the project into steps, or have trouble pacing themselves to meet deadlines.

5. Trouble following multi-step instructions: You might notice your teen forgetting parts of complex instructions or getting confused when trying to complete tasks with multiple steps.

6. Difficulty transitioning between activities: Some teens struggle to shift gears, whether it's moving from one class to another or switching from homework to dinner time.

7. Emotional dysregulation: This can manifest as overreacting to minor setbacks, having trouble calming down after getting upset, or struggling to maintain a positive attitude when faced with challenges.
8. Impulsivity: This might show up as blurting out answers in class, making decisions without thinking through consequences, or having trouble waiting their turn.

It's important to differentiate between typical teenage behavior and potential executive functioning deficits. Occasional forgetfulness or a messy room? Pretty normal. But chronic disorganization, persistent procrastination, and consistent difficulty managing time? Those might indicate deeper issues.

Consider this real-world example: A high school student consistently struggles with homework deadlines. Despite understanding the material, they can't seem to start assignments until the last minute. This leads to incomplete work, lower grades, and increased anxiety. The underlying issue is often a combination of procrastination and poor time management—classic executive functioning challenges.

Or think about a teen who excels in class discussions but struggles with tests and long-term projects. They might have strong cognitive abilities but difficulty with the executive functioning skills needed to study effectively and manage extended tasks.

Another common scenario is the teen who seems to be constantly forgetting things—permission slips, homework assignments, items needed for after-school activities. While everyone forgets things occasionally, consistent forgetfulness across multiple areas of life can indicate challenges with working memory and organization.

It's also worth noting that executive functioning challenges can sometimes masquerade as behavioral issues. A teen who's constantly interrupting others or having emotional outbursts might be struggling with impulse control and emotional regulation—key executive functioning skills.

Understanding these challenges is crucial because it shifts our perspective. Instead of seeing a lazy or defiant teen, we can recognize a young person who's struggling with specific skills—skills that can be improved with the right support and strategies.

In the next section, we'll explore how to identify these challenges in your own teen. Remember, the goal isn't to diagnose or label, but to understand where your teen might need extra support. With this knowledge, you'll be better equipped to help your teen develop the skills they need to thrive.

Identifying Executive Functioning Deficits in Your Teen

So how can you tell if your teen is struggling with executive functioning? Here are some signs to watch for:

- Consistent forgetfulness (completing assignments, losing items, missing deadlines)
- Difficulty following multi-step instructions
- Frequent emotional outbursts
- Trouble starting or completing tasks
- Chronic disorganization (messy backpack, lost papers, cluttered room)
- Poor time management (always running late, underestimating time needed for tasks)
- Difficulty adapting to changes in routine
- Struggles with long-term projects or studying for tests
- Impulsive behavior or decision-making

If you're noticing these signs, don't panic. There are several ways to assess and address executive functioning deficits:

1. Standardized tests: Tools like the Behavior Rating Inventory of Executive Function (BRIEF) can provide detailed insights. These assessments, usually administered by educational

psychologists, measure various aspects of executive functioning and can help pinpoint specific areas of strength and weakness.

2. Behavioral checklists: These allow you to track specific behaviors over time. For example, you might keep a log of how often your teen forgets homework, loses items, or has difficulty starting tasks. Over time, patterns may emerge that can help identify areas of concern.

3. Professional evaluations: Consulting with school counselors, psychologists, or psychiatrists can provide in-depth assessments. These professionals can conduct comprehensive evaluations, including cognitive tests, behavioral observations, and interviews with you and your teen.

4. Self-reflection exercises: Encourage your teen to reflect on their own experiences. Daily behavior logs, where they track their own challenges and successes, can be illuminating. Questionnaires about daily routines, challenges, and feelings can also provide valuable insights.

5. Open discussions: Have honest, non-judgmental conversations with your teen about their experiences. Ask about what parts of school or daily life they find most challenging, and listen carefully to their responses.

6. Teacher feedback: Teachers often have valuable insights into a student's executive functioning skills. They can observe how your teen manages assignments, participates in class, and interacts with peers.

7. Review of school records: Looking at report cards, progress reports, and teacher comments over time can reveal patterns that might indicate executive functioning challenges.

Remember, identifying these challenges isn't about labeling or diagnosing. It's about understanding where your teen needs support so you can help them develop the skills they need to thrive. The goal is to gather information that can guide your efforts to support your teen's growth and success.

It's also important to consider that executive functioning skills exist on a spectrum. Most teens (and adults!) have some areas of strength and some areas that need work. The key is to identify significant challenges that are impacting your teen's daily life and academic success.

If you do identify significant challenges, consider seeking professional help. School counselors can be a good starting point. They can provide initial guidance and may be able to implement support at school. Educational psychologists or neuropsychologists can provide more in-depth evaluations and specific recommendations. For some teens, underlying conditions like attention deficit hyperactivity disorder (ADHD) may be contributing to executive functioning challenges, and a psychiatrist or psychologist can help determine if this is the case.

Struggles with executive functioning don't define your teen. Many brilliant, successful people have wrestled with these skills. The good news is that executive functioning skills can be improved with the right strategies and support. In the next section, we'll explore how you as a parent can play a crucial role in supporting your teen's executive functioning development.

The Role of Parents in Supporting Executive Functioning

As a parent, you play a crucial role in nurturing your teen's executive functioning skills. While specific techniques and strategies will be covered in detail throughout the book, there are several key qualities and approaches you should embody to effectively support your teen:

1. Provide Consistent Support

Be there to guide your teen through challenges. This doesn't mean doing things for them, but rather offering support as they learn to manage tasks independently. The key is to strike a balance between providing assistance and encouraging autonomy. Be available to offer guidance, answer questions, and provide reassurance, but also allow your teen to take the lead in problem-solving and decision-making.

2. Model Good Behaviors

Demonstrate effective organization, time management, and emotional regulation in your own life. Let your teen see you using strategies to manage your responsibilities and handle stress. Explain your thought processes out loud, showing them how you approach complex tasks or challenging situations. This modeling can be a powerful teaching tool, as teens often learn more from what they see than what they're told.

3. Create a Supportive Environment

Foster an atmosphere that encourages the development of executive functioning skills. This goes beyond physical organization to include emotional and social support. Create an environment where it's safe to make mistakes and learn from them. Encourage open communication about challenges and successes. Ensure that your home is a place where your teen feels comfortable practicing and developing these crucial skills.

4. Take a Collaborative Approach

Engage your teen in joint problem-solving and decision-making processes. Instead of imposing solutions, work together to find strategies that work for them. This collaborative approach helps teens feel more invested in their own development and teaches valuable skills in negotiation, compromise, and self-advocacy. It also shows respect for your teen's growing autonomy and capability.

5. Offer Encouragement and Positive Reinforcement

Celebrate efforts and progress, not just outcomes. Provide specific, constructive feedback that focuses on the process rather than just the result. When offering feedback on areas for improvement, focus on specific behaviors and offer suggestions for next time. This approach helps build confidence and resilience, encouraging your teen to persist in developing their skills even when faced with setbacks.

6. Be Patient and Persistent

Remember that developing executive functioning skills is a long-term process. There will be setbacks and frustrations along the way. Stay positive and keep reinforcing good habits, even when progress seems slow. Your consistent support and encouragement are crucial in helping your teen develop these skills over time.

By embodying these qualities and approaches, you create a foundation for your teen's development of executive functioning skills. Your involvement not only helps your teen navigate current challenges but also sets them up for long-term success and independence. The goal is to gradually shift responsibility to your teen as they develop these crucial skills, preparing them for the increasing demands of adolescence and adulthood.

The Importance of Executive Functioning in the Digital Age

Today's teens face challenges that we never had to deal with. The digital age presents unique hurdles to developing executive functioning skills. Consider:

- Screen time management: The constant temptation of smartphones, tablets, and computers can be a major distraction. Teens might find themselves spending hours scrolling through social media or watching videos when they intended to study. This constant engagement can impede their ability to focus, organize, and manage time effectively.

- Digital distractions and multitasking: The pull to juggle multiple digital activities simultaneously is strong. A teen might be texting friends, watching YouTube videos, and attempting homework all at once. This kind of multitasking can fragment attention and reduce the ability to concentrate on any single activity. Research shows that this constant task-switching can lead to decreased efficiency and increased errors (Madore & Wagner, 2019).
- Information overload: The internet provides instant access to a wealth of information, which can be both a blessing and a curse. Teens might struggle to filter relevant information, leading to overwhelm and difficulty prioritizing what's important.
- Social media impact: While social media offers connection and information, it can also be a major source of distraction and stress. The constant influx of updates and the pressure to stay connected can make it difficult for teens to focus on tasks at hand. Additionally, social media can affect self-esteem and emotional regulation, as teens compare themselves to carefully curated online personas.
- Decreased face-to-face interaction: With more communication happening online, teens might have fewer opportunities to practice important social executive functions in person, like reading social cues or managing conversations.
- Instant gratification culture: The digital world often provides immediate rewards (likes, comments, level-ups in games), which can make it harder for teens to persist with longer-term goals that don't provide instant feedback.

But it's not all doom and gloom. Technology also offers tools that can enhance executive functioning skills. Educational apps and digital planners can help teens improve organization, time management, and focus. For example:

- Task management apps like Todoist or Trello can help teens create to-do lists, set deadlines, and prioritize tasks.
- Digital calendars like Google Calendar can help with scheduling and setting reminders.
- Note-taking apps like Evernote or OneNote can assist with organizing study materials and ideas.
- Focus apps like Forest or Freedom can help teens manage screen time and reduce distractions.
- Mindfulness apps like Headspace or Calm can support emotional regulation and stress management.

The key is finding balance. Here are some strategies to help your teen navigate the digital world while developing crucial executive functioning skills:

1. Set clear boundaries: Establish rules around screen time, including tech-free zones (like the dinner table) and times (like an hour before bed).
2. Model good digital habits: Demonstrate healthy technology use yourself. Put your phone away during family time and talk about how you manage your own digital distractions.
3. Encourage tech breaks: Help your teen build in regular breaks from screens. This could include outdoor activities, reading physical books, or engaging in hands-on hobbies.
4. Teach critical thinking skills: Help your teen learn to evaluate online information critically. This can improve their ability to prioritize and manage information overload.
5. Use technology intentionally: Encourage your teen to use technology as a tool rather than a default activity. Help them choose apps and programs that genuinely support their goals and productivity.
6. Practice digital mindfulness: Teach your teen to be aware of their digital habits. Encourage them to notice how they feel after different online activities and to make conscious choices about their tech use.

7. Prioritize face-to-face connections: While online connections are important, make sure your teen has plenty of opportunities for in-person social interactions to practice important social-emotional skills.

8. Leverage educational technology: Explore digital tools designed to support learning and executive functioning. Many schools use platforms like Google Classroom or Microsoft Teams, which can help with organization and task management.

9. Discuss digital citizenship: Talk with your teen about responsible online behavior, including managing their digital footprint and understanding the permanence of online actions.

10. Be flexible and adapt: As technology evolves, be prepared to adjust your approach. Stay informed about new apps and platforms your teen is using and be open to discussing their benefits and potential drawbacks.

By helping your teen navigate these digital challenges and opportunities, you're not just supporting their current academic success—you're preparing them for a future where strong executive functioning skills will be more crucial than ever.

As we wrap up this chapter, remember: Executive functioning skills are the foundation for your teen's success, both now and in the future. By understanding these skills and supporting their development, you're giving your teen a tremendous gift—the ability to navigate life's challenges with confidence and competence.

This is a journey. There will be ups and downs, progress and setbacks. But with patience, persistence, and the right strategies, you can help your teen develop the executive functioning skills they need to thrive in school and in life.

The digital age may present new challenges, but it also offers unprecedented opportunities for growth and learning. By embracing these opportunities while mindfully managing the challenges, we can help our teens develop into capable, confident adults ready to tackle whatever the future holds.

In the next chapter, we'll focus specifically on strategies for improving focus and attention. Get ready to discover practical tools that can transform your teen's ability to concentrate and get things done. The journey to better executive functioning starts here—and the rewards will last a lifetime.

TWO

Getting Organized

You walk into your teen's room and see a sea of papers scattered across the desk, textbooks piled haphazardly, and a calendar that hasn't been updated in weeks. Sound familiar? This chaos often mirrors the internal disorganization many teens feel. But don't worry —we're about to transform that chaos into order.

In this chapter, we'll explore how a simple tool—the daily planner— can be a game-changer for your teen. We'll dive into strategies for creating effective checklists, breaking down daunting tasks into manageable chunks, and even tackle the challenge of digital organization. By the end, you'll have a toolkit to help your teen master the art of organization, reducing stress and boosting productivity along the way.

Organization isn't just about having a tidy room (though that's certainly a bonus). It's about creating systems that help your teen navigate their busy life with confidence and ease. When teens are organized, they're better equipped to handle the demands of school, extracurricular activities, and social life. They're less likely to forget assignments, miss deadlines, or feel overwhelmed by their responsibilities.

But here's the thing: organization doesn't come naturally to everyone. For many teens, it's a skill that needs to be learned and practiced. And that's where you come in. As a parent, you play a crucial role in helping your teen develop these essential skills. Don't worry if you're not the most organized person yourself—we'll guide you through each step of the process.

Throughout this chapter, we'll share practical strategies, real-life examples, and exercises you can do with your teen. We'll address common challenges and offer solutions that you can tailor to your teen's unique needs and preferences. Remember, there's no one-size-fits-all approach to organization. The key is to find what works for your teen and to be patient as they develop these new habits.

So, are you ready to help your teen conquer chaos and embrace order? Let's dive in!

Creating a Daily Planner for Your Teen

A daily planner isn't just a glorified to-do list—it's a comprehensive system for managing time and tasks. Think of it as your teen's personal assistant, keeping track of everything from homework assignments to social events.

Why is a planner so powerful? For starters, it supercharges productivity. When your teen can see at a glance what needs to be done and when, it becomes easier to allocate time effectively and focus on one task at a time. No more multitasking mayhem!

But the benefits go beyond just getting things done. A well-maintained planner can be a stress-buster, breaking down overwhelming work-loads into manageable chunks. It's like having a roadmap for the week—suddenly, that mountain of tasks doesn't seem so insurmountable.

Plus, a planner ensures a balanced life. It's not all about homework and chores; it makes room for fun stuff too. By seeing all their commitments in one place, your teen can strike a healthy balance between work and play.

Now, let's talk about choosing the right planner. It's not one-size-fits-all—the best planner is the one your teen will actually use. Here are some options to consider:

1. Digital apps: Tools like Todoist and Google Calendar are great for tech-savvy teens. They're accessible from any device and often come with handy features like reminders and notifications. If your teen is always glued to their phone, a digital planner might be the way to go.
2. Paper planners: Some teens prefer the tactile experience of writing things down. The act of physically crossing off completed tasks can be incredibly satisfying. Plus, there's no risk of getting distracted by social media notifications when using a paper planner.
3. Bullet journals: For creative types, bullet journals offer a customizable option. Your teen can design a system that fits their specific needs and personality. This method combines planning with artistic expression, which can make organization feel less like a chore and more like a creative outlet.

When setting up the planner, make sure it covers all aspects of your teen's life:

- Academic subjects: Note down homework assignments, project deadlines, and exam dates. Encourage your teen to color-code by subject for easy reference.
- Extracurricular activities: Include sports practices, music lessons, or club meetings. This helps prevent scheduling conflicts and ensures your teen doesn't overcommit.
- Chores and responsibilities: List household tasks to keep your

teen accountable. This teaches valuable life skills and helps them contribute to the family.
- Social events and leisure activities: Because all work and no play... well, you know the rest. Scheduling fun activities gives your teen something to look forward to and helps maintain a healthy work-life balance.

The key to making the planner work? Consistency. Encourage your teen to:

- Conduct daily reviews: A quick check each evening helps them stay on top of tasks and prepares them for the next day. This could become part of their bedtime routine.
- Hold weekly planning sessions: Set aside time each weekend to plan the upcoming week. This is a great opportunity for you to check in with your teen and offer support if needed.
- Incorporate feedback: If something's not working, tweak it. The planner should evolve with your teen's needs. Maybe they realize they need more space for notes, or perhaps they want to add a mood tracker. Be open to adjustments.

Remember, the goal isn't perfection—it's progress. Celebrate the small wins as your teen develops this crucial organizational skill. Did they remember to write down all their assignments this week? That's worth a high five! Did they complete all their tasks for the day? Maybe that earns a small reward.

Here's a practical exercise to get started:

1. Sit down with your teen and create a weekly spread in their planner. Start by filling in fixed commitments like school hours and regular activities. Then, add in homework time, study sessions, and any upcoming deadlines or events. Don't forget to schedule some downtime too!

2. Once you've set up the week, discuss how to use the planner effectively. Show your teen how to prioritize tasks, estimate how long each will take, and schedule accordingly. This is also a great time to talk about the importance of building in buffer time for unexpected tasks or delays.

As your teen gets used to using their planner, you might notice some common challenges. Maybe they forget to check it regularly, or perhaps they struggle to estimate how long tasks will take. These are normal bumps in the road. Work together to find solutions. For example, if they often forget to check their planner, you could set reminders on their phone or leave sticky notes in strategic locations.

Using a planner effectively is a skill that takes time to develop. Be patient with your teen (and yourself!) as you navigate this new system. With consistent use and positive reinforcement, your teen will soon be on their way to becoming a planning pro.

Using Checklists and Templates for Better Organization

Ever feel like your teen is drowning in a sea of tasks? Enter the humble checklist—a simple yet powerful tool for staying afloat.

Checklists are like life rafts in the ocean of responsibilities. They break down big, scary tasks into manageable steps, providing a clear path forward. Each check mark is a mini-victory, boosting confidence and motivation.

Let's say your teen has a science project looming. Without a checklist, it's a vague, daunting monster. But break it down into steps—gather materials, conduct experiments, write the report—and suddenly it's a series of achievable tasks.

Creating effective checklists is an art. Here's how to master it:

1. Categorize tasks: Group similar items together. Academic tasks in one list, personal tasks in another. This helps your

teen focus on one area at a time without feeling overwhelmed by the totality of their responsibilities.

2. Prioritize: Not all tasks are created equal. Teach your teen to identify what's urgent and what can wait. You might introduce them to the Eisenhower Matrix, which categorizes tasks as:
    - Urgent and important (do immediately)
    - Important but not urgent (schedule for later)
    - Urgent but not important (delegate if possible)
    - Neither urgent nor important (eliminate)

3. Set deadlines: A task without a deadline is like a ship without a destination—it'll float aimlessly. Help your teen set realistic deadlines for each item on their checklist.

4. Keep it manageable: Avoid overwhelming lists. Focus on what really needs to get done. A good rule of thumb is to limit daily to-do lists to 3-5 important tasks.

5. Use action verbs: Start each item with a verb to make it clear what needs to be done. For example, "Write introduction for essay" is clearer than "Essay introduction."

6. Break down big tasks: If a task will take more than an hour, break it into smaller subtasks. This makes it less daunting and easier to get started.

Templates are another secret weapon in the organization arsenal. They provide a consistent framework for tackling recurring tasks. Here are some ideas:

- Homework tracking templates: Keep tabs on assignments, due dates, and materials needed. This could include columns for the subject, assignment details, due date, and completion status.
- Project planning templates: Break down big projects into smaller, less intimidating steps. This might include sections for project goals, resources needed, task breakdown, and timeline.

- Daily routine templates: Streamline the day by allocating specific times for study, leisure, and other activities. This helps create structure and ensures important tasks don't fall through the cracks.
- Test preparation templates: Create a structured approach to studying for exams. This could include sections for key topics, practice questions, and areas that need more focus.
- Book report templates: For avid readers or English class assignments, a template can help organize thoughts and ensure all necessary elements are covered.

The beauty of templates is that they're customizable. Encourage your teen to tailor them to their specific needs and preferences. A template for a math whiz might look different from one for a budding artist— and that's okay!

Here's a practical exercise to get your teen started with checklists and templates:

1. Choose an upcoming assignment or project.
2. Sit down with your teen and brainstorm all the steps needed to complete it.
3. Organize these steps into a checklist, grouping related tasks and putting them in a logical order.
4. Add deadlines to each item.
5. Create a template based on this checklist that can be used for similar future assignments.

As your teen uses these tools, they might encounter some challenges. Maybe they struggle to break tasks down into small enough steps, or perhaps they have trouble estimating how long each task will take. These are common issues that improve with practice. Encourage your teen to reflect on what's working and what isn't, and adjust their approach accordingly.

Remember, the goal of checklists and templates isn't to create more work, but to make existing work more manageable. They should simplify life, not complicate it. If your teen finds that a particular checklist or template isn't helping, it's okay to ditch it and try something else.

With consistent use, checklists and templates can become powerful allies in your teen's quest for organization. They provide structure, reduce stress, and give a satisfying sense of progress. Plus, they're skills that will serve your teen well beyond their school years, into college and their future career.

Breaking Down Tasks: The Power of Micro-Goals

Picture this: Your teen is staring at a massive research paper assignment, feeling overwhelmed and unsure where to start. Sound familiar? This is where micro-goals come to the rescue.

Micro-goals are like stepping stones across a rushing river of tasks. Instead of trying to leap across in one bound (and likely falling in), your teen can take small, manageable steps.

Here's why micro-goals are so powerful:

1. They crush procrastination: Big tasks are scary. Small tasks? Not so much. By breaking things down, your teen is more likely to get started. It's much easier to face "write the introduction paragraph" than "write a 10-page paper."
2. They boost motivation: Each completed micro-goal is a win. And wins feel good, spurring your teen on to the next task. This creates a positive feedback loop, where success breeds more success.
3. They build confidence: As your teen checks off micro-goals, they see tangible progress. This reinforces their ability to tackle challenges and builds self-efficacy.

4. They improve focus: Working on small, specific tasks makes it easier to concentrate. Your teen can give their full attention to one manageable piece at a time, rather than feeling scattered by the enormity of the whole project.

5. They reduce overwhelm: Breaking a big task into smaller parts makes it feel less daunting. This can significantly reduce stress and anxiety associated with large projects.

So, how do you implement micro-goals? Let's break it down (see what we did there?):

1. Start by chunking: Take that big assignment and divide it into smaller parts. Research, outline, draft, revise—each becomes its own micro-goal.

2. Set short-term milestones: Instead of "finish the project by Friday," try "complete research by Tuesday, outline by Wednesday," and so on. This creates a clear timeline and helps prevent last-minute rushes.

3. Make it visual: Use a checklist or progress bar to track micro-goals. Seeing progress can be incredibly motivating. You might use a simple to-do list, a project management app, or even a physical chart on the wall.

4. Prioritize: Not all micro-goals are created equal. Help your teen identify which tasks are most crucial and should be tackled first.

5. Estimate time: Encourage your teen to guess how long each micro-goal will take. This helps with time management and gets easier with practice.

6. Build in rewards: Consider setting up small rewards for completing micro-goals. This could be as simple as a short break, a favorite snack, or some screen time.

Let's put this into practice with a common task: writing a research paper.

Instead of one daunting task, it becomes a series of manageable micro-goals:

1. Choose a topic
2. Gather sources (find 5 reliable sources)
3. Take notes on each source
4. Create an outline
5. Write the introduction
6. Write the first body paragraph
7. Write the second body paragraph
8. Write the third body paragraph
9. Write the conclusion
10. Create a bibliography
11. Revise and edit
12. Proofread

Each of these steps is less intimidating than "write a research paper," making it easier for your teen to get started and maintain momentum.

To help your teen start using micro-goals:

1. Choose an upcoming project or assignment.
2. Brainstorm all the steps needed to complete it. Encourage your teen to be as specific as possible.
3. Organize these steps in a logical order.
4. For each step, discuss:
   - How long might this take?
   - What resources are needed?
   - Are there any potential obstacles?
5. Create a timeline for completing each micro-goal.
6. Decide how progress will be tracked (checklist, app, chart, etc.).

As your teen starts working with micro-goals, they might face some challenges. Maybe they struggle to break tasks down small enough, or perhaps they underestimate how long each step will take. These are normal hurdles that get easier with practice. Encourage your teen to reflect on what's working and what isn't, and adjust their approach as needed.

Remember, the goal isn't just to complete the task—it's to build skills and confidence along the way. As your teen masters the art of micro-goals, they'll develop a growth mindset, seeing challenges as opportunities rather than obstacles.

Micro-goals can be applied to all sorts of tasks beyond schoolwork too. Cleaning a messy room becomes less daunting when broken down into "pick up clothes," "organize desk," "vacuum floor," etc. Even personal goals like learning a new skill can benefit from this approach.

By embracing micro-goals, your teen is learning a valuable life skill that will serve them well beyond their school years. They're developing the ability to tackle complex projects, manage their time effectively, and persist in the face of challenges. These are skills that will be invaluable in college, in their future career, and in life in general.

So the next time your teen feels overwhelmed by a big task, remind them: no mountain is climbed in a single leap. It's conquered one step at a time. With micro-goals, they have the tools to start that climb—and reach the summit.

Developing Long-Term Planning Skills

Long-term planning is like charting a course for an epic journey. It's about looking beyond the day-to-day and setting a direction for the future. For teens, this might involve academic goals like improving their GPA or personal goals like learning a new skill.

Developing long-term planning skills is crucial for several reasons:

1. It provides direction: Long-term goals give your teen something to work towards, providing motivation and purpose.
2. It teaches prioritization: When your teen has a clear long-term goal, it's easier to decide what's important and what's not.
3. It builds resilience: Long-term planning involves overcoming obstacles and adapting to changes, which builds important life skills.
4. It prepares for the future: Whether it's college applications or career planning, long-term thinking is essential for future success.

Here's how to help your teen set and achieve long-term goals:

1. Make it SMART: Teach your teen to set Specific, Measurable, Achievable, Relevant, and Time-bound goals. Instead of "do better in math," try "improve math grade from C to B by the end of the semester." For example:
   ◦ Specific: Improve math grade
   ◦ Measurable: From C to B
   ◦ Achievable: Moving up one grade level is realistic
   ◦ Relevant: Better grades align with college admission goals
   ◦ Time-bound: By the end of the semester
2. Create a roadmap: Break the goal down into actionable steps. If the goal is to improve in math, steps might include:
   ◦ Complete all homework on time
   ◦ Attend weekly study sessions
   ◦ Seek help from a tutor once a month
   ◦ Practice extra problems for 30 minutes each day
   ◦ Review notes for 15 minutes after each class
3. Set milestones: These are like checkpoints on the journey. They help track progress and provide opportunities to

celebrate small wins along the way. For our math example, milestones might be:

- ○ Achieve a B on the next quiz
- ○ Maintain a B average for a month
- ○ Improve test scores by 10%

4. Make it visual: Create a timeline or use a goal-tracking app to visualize the path to success. This could be a simple chart on the wall or a digital progress bar. Seeing progress can be incredibly motivating.

5. Review and adjust: Life happens, and plans may need to change. Encourage regular check-ins to review progress and make adjustments as needed. Maybe your teen realizes they need more tutoring than initially thought, or perhaps they're progressing faster than expected and can set more ambitious goals.

Tools for tracking long-term goals:

- Progress journals: Encourage your teen to write regular entries about their achievements and challenges. This not only tracks progress but also promotes self-reflection and problem-solving.
- Tracking apps: Apps like Trello or Asana can help manage goals and deadlines. These tools allow for easy updating and can send reminders to keep your teen on track.
- Vision boards: A visual representation of goals can be a powerful motivator. This could be a physical board with images and words representing their goals, or a digital collage they can set as their computer background.

Long-term planning workshop:

1. Identify a long-term goal: Have your teen choose something they want to achieve in the next 6-12 months.

2. Make it SMART: Work together to refine the goal using the SMART criteria.
3. Create a roadmap: Break the goal down into smaller steps and milestones.
4. Choose a tracking method: Decide how progress will be monitored (journal, app, chart, etc.).
5. Schedule regular check-ins: Set dates for reviewing progress and making adjustments.

As your teen works on their long-term goal, they might encounter some challenges:

- Losing motivation: It's normal for enthusiasm to wane over time. Encourage your teen to reconnect with their 'why' - the reason they set this goal in the first place.
- Unexpected obstacles: Life rarely goes exactly as planned. Help your teen see obstacles as learning opportunities rather than failures.
- Changing priorities: Sometimes, goals that seemed important at first become less so over time. It's okay to reassess and change course if needed.

Remember, developing long-term planning skills is a process. It takes practice, patience, and sometimes a bit of trial and error. But with your support, your teen can learn to set and achieve meaningful goals, building confidence and life skills along the way.

Long-term planning isn't just about achieving specific goals - it's about developing a forward-thinking mindset. As your teen practices these skills, they'll become better at anticipating challenges, seizing opportunities, and shaping their own future.

Decluttering: Strategies for a Clean and Organized Space

A cluttered space often leads to a cluttered mind. Helping your teen create and maintain an organized environment can have a big impact on their focus, productivity, and overall well-being.

Here's why a clean space matters:

1. Improved focus: Less visual distraction means better concentration. When your teen's workspace is clear, their mind can focus on the task at hand rather than being pulled in multiple directions by surrounding clutter.
2. Reduced stress: A tidy environment can help calm a busy mind. Coming home to a neat room can be a relief after a long day at school, rather than another source of stress.
3. Better time management: No more wasting time searching for lost items! When everything has a place, your teen can spend their energy on important tasks rather than hunting for missing homework or that elusive permission slip.
4. Increased productivity: An organized space streamlines work processes. With all necessary materials at hand and distractions minimized, your teen can work more efficiently.
5. Improved sleep: A clutter-free bedroom can contribute to better sleep quality. It's easier to relax and unwind in a tidy space.

So, how do you help your teen declutter? Here's a step-by-step approach:

1. Sort it out: Help your teen go through their belongings, sorting items into three categories: keep, donate, and discard. This can be a big job, so consider tackling one area at a time - start with the desk, then move to the closet, and so on.
2. Organize what's left: Use bins, shelves, and drawers to give everything a home. Label storage areas to make it easy to

remember where things go. Consider using clear containers so items are visible at a glance.

3. Maintain the system: Establish regular clean-up routines. A quick 10-minute tidy at the end of each day can work wonders. Make it a habit - perhaps while listening to a favorite song or podcast to make it more enjoyable.
4. Do periodic purges: Every few months, encourage your teen to reassess their belongings and let go of what they no longer need. This prevents clutter from building up over time.

Creating a dedicated homework station can be a game-changer. Here's how:

1. Choose the right location: Find a quiet spot with good lighting and minimal distractions. This could be a corner of their bedroom, a spot in the family room, or even a converted closet.
2. Stock it with essentials: Pens, paper, calculator, computer— whatever your teen needs for their studies. Keep frequently used items within easy reach.
3. Keep it organized: Use desk organizers, file folders, and other tools to keep supplies tidy and accessible. A pegboard or bulletin board can be great for hanging up schedules, reminders, and inspirational quotes.
4. Minimize distractions: Consider using a white noise machine or noise-canceling headphones to create a focused environment. If the homework station is in a shared space, a folding screen can help create a sense of privacy.
5. Make it personal: Let your teen add some personal touches to make the space feel inviting. This could be artwork, photos, or a small plant.

Kickstart the decluttering process:

1. Choose one area to focus on - let's say the desk.
2. Remove everything from the desk and wipe it clean.
3. Sort through the items, deciding what to keep, donate, or discard.
4. For the items being kept, decide where each one belongs. Does it need to be on the desk, or can it be stored elsewhere?
5. Put things back, with the most frequently used items in easy reach.
6. Maintain the new organization by spending 5 minutes each evening putting things back in their place.

As your teen goes through this process, they might face some challenges:

- Emotional attachment to items: It can be hard to let go of things, even if they're no longer useful. Encourage your teen to consider whether each item truly adds value to their life.
- Feeling overwhelmed: Decluttering can seem like a huge task. Break it down into smaller, manageable chunks - maybe tackle one drawer or shelf at a time.
- Maintaining the new system: Old habits can be hard to break. Gentle reminders and positive reinforcement can help your teen stick to their new organizational habits.

Remember, the goal is to create a space that supports your teen's productivity and well-being. It might take some trial and error to find the perfect setup, but the payoff in improved focus and reduced stress is worth it.

A clutter-free space isn't just about tidiness - it's about creating an environment that supports your teen's goals and reduces unnecessary stress. By helping your teen master the art of decluttering, you're giving them valuable skills that will serve them well throughout their life.

Organizing Digital Files and Schoolwork

In today's digital age, managing electronic files is just as important as organizing physical spaces. A well-organized digital system can save time, reduce stress, and improve efficiency.

Here's why digital organization matters:

1. Quick access to information: No more frantic searching for that one document! With a good system, your teen can find what they need in seconds.
2. Reduced digital clutter: A tidy digital space can be as calming as a tidy physical space. It reduces mental load and makes working on the computer more pleasant.
3. Improved collaboration: Organized files make it easier to share and work with others. This is especially important for group projects or when submitting work to teachers.
4. Better backup and security: When files are organized, it's easier to ensure everything important is backed up properly.

Steps to create a digital filing system:

1. Categorize subjects: Create main folders for each subject or class. For example: Math, English, Science, History, etc.
2. Use subfolders: Within each main folder, create subfolders for assignments, notes, projects, etc. This might look like: Math > Homework Math > Notes Math > Tests Math > Projects
3. Develop a naming convention: Use consistent, descriptive file names. For example: "2023-09-15_History_Essay_Draft1" This system includes the date, subject, type of assignment, and version, making it easy to find and identify files at a glance.

4. Use tags or colors: Many file systems allow for tagging or color-coding. This can be useful for marking priority items or categorizing across subjects (e.g., all essays could be tagged "essay" regardless of subject).

5. Clean up regularly: Just like physical spaces, digital spaces need regular decluttering. Set aside time each week or month to delete unnecessary files and organize new ones.

Useful tools and apps:

- Google Drive: Great for cloud storage and collaboration. It integrates well with Google Docs, Sheets, and Slides, which many schools use.
- OneNote: Excellent for note-taking and organization. It allows for the creation of notebooks, sections, and pages, mimicking a physical notebook structure.
- Evernote: Powerful for tagging and categorizing notes. It's especially good for collecting research from various sources.
- Dropbox: Another cloud storage option that's good for syncing files across devices.
- Notion: A versatile tool that can be used for note-taking, project management, and more. It's highly customizable, which can be great for teens who like to design their own systems.

Maintenance tips:

1. Weekly file reviews: Set aside time each week to organize new files and delete unnecessary ones. This could be part of the weekly planning session we discussed earlier.

2. Regular backups: Use an external hard drive or cloud service to protect against data loss. Teach your teen the importance of backing up their work regularly.

3. Update and evolve: As your teen's needs change, be ready to

adjust the system. What works in freshman year might need tweaking by senior year.

4. Use the search function: Teach your teen how to use file search effectively. Even with the best organization system, sometimes it's faster to search for a file by name.

Here's a practical exercise to get your teen started with digital organization:

1. Choose one subject or project to organize.
2. Create a main folder for that subject.
3. Brainstorm the types of files that will go in this folder (homework, notes, projects, etc.) and create subfolders accordingly.
4. Go through existing files related to this subject and move them into the appropriate subfolders.
5. Rename files as needed to fit the new naming convention.
6. Delete any unnecessary or duplicate files.

As your teen implements their digital organization system, they might encounter some challenges:

- Consistency: It can be tempting to slip back into old habits. Encourage your teen to stick with their new system, even when they're in a hurry.
- Overcomplication: Sometimes, in an effort to be organized, we can create systems that are too complex. If your teen finds they're spending more time organizing than working, it might be time to simplify.
- Digital hoarding: Just like with physical items, it can be hard to delete digital files. Encourage your teen to regularly assess what they truly need to keep.

Remember, the goal is to create a digital organization system that works for your teen. It might take some experimentation to find the right setup, but the result will be a more efficient and less stressful digital life.

By mastering digital organization, your teen is developing skills that will serve them well in college and beyond. In our increasingly digital world, the ability to manage information effectively is a crucial skill for success.

Real-Life Case Study: From Chaos to Order

Meet Emma, a bright high school sophomore struggling with organization. Her room was a whirlwind of crumpled papers and forgotten assignments. Despite her intelligence, Emma's grades were slipping, and her stress levels were sky-high.

When we first met Emma, her parents, Sarah and Tom, were at their wits' end. They knew their daughter was capable of so much more, but her disorganization was holding her back. Emma would often miss deadlines, forget about tests until the last minute, and struggle to find important papers in her messy backpack.

Here's how we helped Emma turn things around:

1. Introduced daily planning: We started by helping Emma choose a planner that suited her style. She opted for a colorful paper planner with plenty of space for notes. We taught her how to use it effectively, scheduling not just homework but also extracurricular activities and downtime.
2. Implemented checklists and templates: We created checklists for common tasks like packing her backpack and preparing for tests. We also developed templates for assignments she frequently encountered, like book reports and math problem sets.
3. Set up a homework station: We designated a quiet corner of Emma's room as her study space. We equipped it with good lighting, comfortable seating, and all the supplies she might

need. Everything had its place, from pens and highlighters to textbooks and notebooks.

4. Developed a digital organization system: Emma learned to categorize and name her digital files consistently. We set up a folder structure in Google Drive that mirrored her school subjects, making it easy to file and find documents.

5. Introduced micro-goals: For larger projects, we taught Emma to break them down into smaller, manageable tasks. This helped her overcome procrastination and made big assignments feel less overwhelming.

The journey wasn't always smooth. We had to adjust strategies along the way:

- We simplified overly detailed checklists that were becoming overwhelming. Emma found that she didn't need to write down every single step; a more general checklist worked better for her.
- We set a specific time each evening for Emma to update her planner. Initially, she would forget to use it, but by tying it to another habit (checking her phone before bed), it became routine.
- We experimented with different digital tools until we found the ones that worked best for her. Emma discovered she preferred Google Drive to Dropbox, and that she loved using the notes app.

The results were remarkable:

- Emma's grades improved significantly. She went from mostly Cs to As and Bs within a semester.
- She became more proactive about starting assignments, often beginning projects well before their due dates.
- Her parents noticed she seemed less stressed and more in

control. The frantic searches for lost papers became a thing of the past.

- Emma's confidence grew as she saw herself succeeding. She started taking on leadership roles in her extracurricular activities, applying the organizational skills she had learned.
- Her teachers commented on the improvement in her work quality and her increased participation in class.

Perhaps most importantly, Emma felt a sense of control over her life that she hadn't experienced before. She was proud of her newfound skills and eager to keep improving.

Emma's story shows that with the right strategies and support, any teen can develop strong organizational skills. It's not about perfection —it's about progress. Emma still has moments of forgetfulness or disorganization, but now she has the tools to get back on track quickly.

For parents reading this, remember that change takes time. Be patient with your teen (and yourself!) as you implement new organizational strategies. Celebrate small victories along the way, and don't get discouraged by setbacks. With consistency and positive reinforcement, you can help your teen transform chaos into order, setting the stage for success in school and beyond.

As we wrap up this chapter, remember that organization is a skill that can be learned and improved over time. With patience, consistency, and the right tools, your teen can transform chaos into order, setting the stage for success in school and beyond.

In the next chapter, we'll explore strategies for effective time management, helping your teen balance schoolwork, extracurriculars, and personal time. Get ready to discover how to make the most of every hour in the day!

THREE

Time Management Techniques

Your teen is juggling school assignments, soccer practice, and social commitments, all while trying to squeeze in some much-needed downtime. It's like watching a circus performer spinning plates—at any moment, one might come crashing down. Sound familiar?

Time management isn't just about getting things done; it's about getting the right things done efficiently. In this chapter, we'll dive into strategies that can help your teen master the art of time management, reducing stress and boosting productivity along the way.

But before we jump in, let's take a moment to consider why time management is so crucial for teens. In today's fast-paced world, teens are under more pressure than ever before. They're expected to excel academically, participate in extracurricular activities, maintain a social life, and possibly even hold down a part-time job. Without effective time management skills, it's all too easy for them to become overwhelmed, stressed, and burnt out.

Moreover, the habits they form now will likely stick with them into adulthood. By helping your teen develop strong time management skills, you're not just setting them up for success in high school—you're equipping them with tools they'll use throughout college, in their future careers, and in their personal lives.

So, are you ready to help your teen transform from a frazzled juggler to a master of time? Let's get started!

Understanding Time Management

Think of time management as your teen's personal superpower. It's not just about completing homework on time—it's about efficiently using time to balance schoolwork, extracurricular activities, social life, and personal interests. When teens master this skill, they can:

1. Efficiently use time: Giving each task the attention it deserves without feeling rushed. This means your teen can focus fully on their math homework without worrying about the English essay they need to write next.
2. Prioritize tasks: Determining which activities are most important and tackling them first. For instance, finishing a project due tomorrow takes precedence over studying for a test next week.
3. Balance multiple responsibilities: Allocating time among various activities without feeling overwhelmed. This could mean dedicating two hours to homework, one hour to soccer practice, and still having time left over for a video chat with friends.

But here's the catch: Even the most well-intentioned plans can go off the rails. Common pitfalls include:

- Underestimating task durations: That "quick" assignment suddenly takes three hours instead of one. This is a common issue for teens who haven't yet developed a realistic sense of how long tasks take.

- Overcommitting to activities: Trying to do it all and ending up burnt out. Many teens, in their enthusiasm, sign up for too many clubs or take on too many responsibilities.
- Lack of prioritization: Spending too much time on less critical tasks, leaving important ones incomplete or rushed. For example, a teen might spend hours perfecting the formatting of an essay while neglecting the content.

These pitfalls can lead to a vicious cycle of stress, procrastination, and poor performance. But don't worry—awareness is the first step to prevention, and we'll cover strategies to avoid these traps.

Mastering time management brings a host of benefits:

1. Reduced stress: When teens manage their time effectively, they're less likely to feel overwhelmed. No more panicked late-night study sessions or frantic rushes to complete assignments.
2. Improved academic performance: With proper time allocation, teens can dedicate appropriate time to studying and assignments. This often leads to better grades and a deeper understanding of the material.
3. More free time: Efficient handling of responsibilities creates space for hobbies and relaxation. Your teen might find they have time for that book they've been wanting to read or that new hobby they've been curious about.
4. Better sleep habits: Good time management often leads to more regular sleep patterns, as late-night cramming sessions become a thing of the past.
5. Increased confidence: As teens see themselves consistently meeting deadlines and achieving goals, their self-confidence grows.

So, how do we assess your teen's current time management skills? Try these methods:

1. Daily activity logs: Encourage your teen to record how they spend their time each day. This can be an eye-opening exercise, revealing where time is being well-spent and where it's being wasted.
2. Self-reflection questionnaires: Ask questions about daily routines and time management challenges. For example: "Do you often feel rushed?" or "How often do you complete assignments at the last minute?"
3. Teacher feedback: Get insights into how your teen manages time in a school setting. Teachers can provide valuable observations about your teen's ability to meet deadlines and stay focused in class.

Here's a practical tool to get started.

Time Management Assessment Worksheet:

1. Daily Activity Log: Record how you spend each hour for one week. Be honest—include everything from classes and homework to social media scrolling and TV watching.
2. Self-Reflection Questions:
   - What activities take up most of your time?
   - Do you feel rushed or stressed while completing tasks?
   - Which tasks do you often leave unfinished?
   - How often do you procrastinate, and on what types of tasks?
   - Do you have a system for prioritizing your work?
3. Teacher Feedback: Ask your teachers about your time management skills. Consider questions like:
   - Do I consistently turn in assignments on time?
   - How well do I manage long-term projects?
   - Do I seem focused and engaged during class?

4. Identifying Improvements: Based on your logs, self-reflection, and teacher feedback, list three areas where you can improve your time management. Set specific, achievable goals for each area.

By using this worksheet, your teen can take an active role in assessing and improving their time management skills. This self-awareness is the first step towards positive change.

Remember, the goal isn't perfection. We're not aiming to turn your teen into a robot, rigidly adhering to a minute-by-minute schedule. Instead, we want to help them develop a flexible, personalized approach to managing their time effectively. This might involve some trial and error, and that's okay. The important thing is to start the process and keep refining it over time.

In the next section, we'll explore a powerful technique that can revolutionize the way your teen approaches tasks and manages their time. Get ready to learn about the Pomodoro Technique!

The Pomodoro Technique for Teens

Ever heard of the Pomodoro Technique? It's like interval training for your brain. Developed by Francesco Cirillo in the late 1980s, this method involves breaking work into focused 25-minute sessions (called "Pomodoros"), separated by short breaks.

Here's why it works:

1. Enhances focus: Short, intense work periods help maintain concentration. It's easier to stay focused when you know a break is coming soon.
2. Reduces burnout: Regular breaks prevent mental fatigue. These short pauses give the brain a chance to rest and recharge.

3. Balances work and rest: Creates a rhythm that keeps your teen productive without feeling overwhelmed. It's like a dance between effort and relaxation.
4. Makes big tasks less daunting: Breaking work into 25-minute chunks makes even the largest projects feel manageable.
5. Helps track productivity: By counting Pomodoros, your teen can see how much time they're actually spending on tasks.

Implementing the Pomodoro Technique is straightforward:

1. Choose a task to focus on. This could be homework, studying for a test, or working on a project.
2. Set a timer for 25 minutes. This is one Pomodoro.
3. Work on the task until the timer rings. During this time, focus solely on the chosen task. No checking phones or social media!
4. Take a 5-minute break. Use this time to stretch, grab a snack, or do something relaxing.
5. After four Pomodoros, take a longer break (15-30 minutes). This extended break helps prevent burnout and keeps your teen refreshed.

The beauty of this technique is its flexibility. Your teen can adjust the intervals based on their needs and attention span. Some might prefer 20-minute work sessions, while others might stretch to 30 minutes. The key is to find a rhythm that works for them.

Here's how your teen might use the Pomodoro Technique for a typical homework session:

- Pomodoro 1 (25 minutes): Start math homework
- 5-minute break: Quick stretch and grab a glass of water
- Pomodoro 2 (25 minutes): Continue math homework
- 5-minute break: Check phone messages
- Pomodoro 3 (25 minutes): Begin English essay

- 5-minute break: Listen to a favorite song
- Pomodoro 4 (25 minutes): Continue English essay
- 30-minute break: Have dinner and relax

Tools to help:

- Pomodoro timer apps (like Tomato Timer or Tide): These apps make it easy to track Pomodoros and breaks.
- Physical timers (yes, even a kitchen timer works!): Some teens might prefer the tactile experience of setting a physical timer.
- Pomodoro logs to track progress: Keeping a log can help your teen see patterns in their productivity and make adjustments as needed.

Here's a simple Pomodoro example log your teen can replicate:

Date	Task	# of Pomodoros	Notes
5/1	Math HW	3	Finished all problems, felt focused
5/1	English Essay	2	Good start, need 2 more Pomodoros to finish

Encouraging your teen to keep a log like this can help them understand their work patterns and improve their time estimates for future tasks.

Some teens might resist the idea of such structured work sessions at first. If this happens, encourage them to try it for just one week. Often, once they experience the benefits—like improved focus and less procrastination—they're more willing to stick with it.

Remember, the Pomodoro Technique isn't meant to be rigid. If your teen is in a great flow state when the timer goes off, it's okay to extend the session. The goal is to create a sustainable work rhythm, not to interrupt productive work unnecessarily.

By breaking work into manageable chunks with regular breaks, your teen can maintain focus, reduce burnout, and achieve a better balance between work and rest. It's a simple yet powerful tool in the time management toolkit.

Breaking Tasks into Manageable Steps

Imagine your teen staring at a massive research paper, feeling overwhelmed before they've even started. Sound familiar? This is where breaking tasks into smaller steps comes in handy.

Why it works:

1. Reduces overwhelm: Transforms daunting projects into a series of achievable actions. Instead of facing a mountain, your teen sees a series of small hills.
2. Increases focus: Allows concentration on one small step at a time. It's easier to focus on "find three sources for the research paper" than "write a 10-page paper."
3. Facilitates progress tracking: Provides visible milestones, boosting motivation. Checking off completed steps gives a sense of accomplishment and momentum.
4. Improves time management: Smaller steps make it easier to estimate how long tasks will take and fit them into available time slots.
5. Enhances quality: By focusing on one step at a time, your teen can give each aspect of the project the attention it deserves.

Here's how to break down tasks effectively:

1. Chunking: Divide larger tasks into smaller, self-contained units. For a research paper, chunks might include research, outlining, writing, and editing.
2. Use checklists: Create a step-by-step list for multi-step

projects. This provides a clear roadmap and the satisfaction of checking off completed items.

3. Set mini-deadlines: Break the overall deadline into smaller, manageable timeframes. This creates a sense of urgency for each step and prevents last-minute rushing.
4. Prioritize steps: Determine which steps are most critical or time-sensitive and tackle those first.
5. Estimate time for each step: This helps with overall time management and scheduling.

Let's apply this to different types of tasks:

Academic projects: For a research paper due in three weeks:

- Week 1: Research and gather sources (2-3 days), Create outline (1-2 days)
- Week 2: Write first draft (3-4 days), Revise and edit (2-3 days)
- Week 3: Write final draft (2-3 days), Proofread and format (1-2 days)

Household chores: Cleaning a messy room:

1. Pick up and put away clothes (15 minutes)
2. Clear and organize desk (20 minutes)
3. Make bed (5 minutes)
4. Vacuum floor (10 minutes)
5. Dust surfaces (10 minutes)

Personal goals: Starting a fitness routine:

1. Research exercises suitable for your fitness level (1 day)
2. Create a weekly workout schedule (30 minutes)
3. Prepare workout clothes and equipment (30 minutes)
4. Start with a 15-minute workout 3 times a week (Week 1)
5. Gradually increase duration and frequency (Weeks 2-4)

6. Track progress and adjust routine as needed (Ongoing)

Remember, flexibility is key. Regularly check in on progress and be ready to adjust the plan if needed. Sometimes, steps might take longer than anticipated or new steps might need to be added. That's okay! The goal is progress, not perfection.

As always, celebrate small victories along the way—they're fuel for motivation! Each completed step is a win and deserves recognition. This could be as simple as a self-high five or a small reward like 10 minutes of video game time.

Here's a practical tool to help your teen break down tasks:

Task Breakdown Worksheet:

1. Task Description: Describe the overall task or project.
2. Final Deadline: When does this need to be completed?
3. Step 1: Identify the first sub-task and set a mini-deadline.
4. Step 2: Identify the second sub-task and set a mini-deadline.
5. Continue until the entire task is broken down.
6. Resources Needed: List any materials, information, or help required for each step.
7. Progress Tracking: Use checkboxes or a progress bar for each step.
8. Adjustments: Note any changes needed and adjust deadlines as necessary.

By using this worksheet, your teen can visualize the breakdown of tasks, making them more manageable and less daunting. It also serves as a central place to track progress and make adjustments as needed.

Encouraging your teen to use this method consistently can lead to improved time management skills, reduced stress, and better project outcomes. It's a valuable skill that will serve them well beyond their school years, into college and their future careers.

Overcoming Procrastination: Practical Tools

Ah, procrastination—the arch-nemesis of productivity. It's the act of delaying or postponing tasks, often to the point where it becomes problematic. Teens frequently struggle with this for various reasons:

- Feeling overwhelmed by the size or complexity of a task
- Lack of clear direction or understanding of how to start
- Fear of failure or perfectionism
- Distractions from technology or social activities
- Low energy or motivation

The impact? Missed deadlines, incomplete assignments, lower grades, and a whole lot of stress. Procrastination can create a vicious cycle where the more a teen puts things off, the more stressed they become, leading to even more procrastination.

But fear not! There are strategies to combat procrastination:

1. The "Eat That Frog" technique: This method, popularized by Brian Tracy, suggests tackling the most challenging task first. It's like ripping off a Band-Aid—once it's done, everything else feels easier in comparison. Why it works:
   - Builds momentum for the rest of the day
   - Eliminates the anxiety of having a big task looming over you
   - Takes advantage of higher energy levels earlier in the day
2. The "Two-Minute Rule": If a task takes two minutes or less, do it immediately. It's amazing how many small tasks we put off that could be quickly knocked out. This rule:
   - Prevents small tasks from piling up
   - Creates a sense of immediate accomplishment
   - Builds the habit of taking immediate action

3. Create a distraction-free environment: Clear the study area of smartphones, social media notifications, and other attention-grabbers. This might involve:
   ○ Using website blockers during study time
   ○ Putting phones in another room
   ○ Finding a quiet space away from TV or family activity
4. Use positive reinforcement: Reward your teen for completing tasks on time. It could be praise, a small treat, or some extra leisure time. This:
   ○ Associates task completion with positive feelings
   ○ Motivates continued productive behavior
   ○ Acknowledges and celebrates effort and progress

Behavioral strategies can also help:

- Accountability partners: Pair your teen with a friend or family member who checks in on their progress. This adds a social element to task completion and can increase motivation.
- Time-blocking: Set specific time slots for focused work on particular tasks. This creates a sense of structure and can make large tasks feel more manageable.
- Visualization: Encourage your teen to visualize how they'll feel when the task is complete. This can help overcome initial resistance to starting.
- The "5-Second Rule": Coined by Mel Robbins, this involves counting backwards from 5 and then taking immediate action.

And don't forget about tools and apps:

- To-do list apps like Todoist or Wunderlist: These help organize tasks and provide a clear view of what needs to be done.
- Focus apps such as Forest or Focus@Will: These apps can

block distracting websites or provide background noise to enhance concentration.
- Habit-tracking apps like Habitica or Streaks: These gamify the process of building good habits and breaking procrastination cycles.

Real-life example: Jake, a high school student, often found himself overwhelmed and cramming at the last minute. Here's how he turned things around:

1. He started using the "Eat That Frog" technique, tackling his most challenging subject (math) first thing after school.
2. Jake used the Forest app to maintain focus, setting it for 25-minute intervals (combining it with the Pomodoro Technique).
3. He found an accountability partner in his friend Sarah. They would check in with each other every evening to ensure they were on track with their tasks.
4. For long-term projects, Jake broke them down into smaller steps and set mini-deadlines for each.

The result? Jake saw a significant improvement in his productivity and a reduction in stress levels. His grades improved, and he found he had more free time to enjoy his hobbies.

Remember, overcoming procrastination is a process. It takes time to build new habits and break old ones. Encourage your teen to be patient with themselves and to keep trying different strategies until they find what works best for them.

Managing Deadlines: Avoiding Last-Minute Rush

Meeting deadlines isn't just about pleasing teachers—it's a life skill that sets the foundation for future success and reduces stress. When teens consistently meet deadlines, they:

- Prevent the vicious cycle of procrastination
- Build confidence and self-esteem
- Create a disciplined routine that serves them well in future academic and professional endeavors
- Reduce stress and anxiety associated with last-minute rushes
- Improve the quality of their work by allowing time for review and revision

Here's a powerful strategy to help your teen stay on track: backward planning.

How it works:

1. Start with the end goal (the deadline)
2. Work backward to identify the steps needed to achieve it
3. Set mini-deadlines for each step

For example, if your teen has a research paper due in four weeks:

- Week 4: Final paper due
- Week 3: Complete final draft, proofread and format
- Week 2: Write first draft, gather feedback
- Week 1: Research and create outline

This approach helps break the project into manageable chunks and ensures steady progress towards the final deadline.

Tools for tracking deadlines:

1. Digital calendars (like Google Calendar):
    - Great for color-coding different types of tasks
    - Can set reminders at various intervals before a deadline
    - Accessible from multiple devices
    - Easy to share with parents or study groups

2. Physical planners or wall calendars:
   - Some teens find writing things down helps reinforce their commitments
   - Provides a visual representation of the month ahead
   - Can be satisfying to physically cross off completed tasks
3. Project management apps (like Trello or Asana):
   - Useful for breaking down larger projects into smaller tasks
   - Can set deadlines for individual components of a project
   - Allows for easy collaboration on group projects
4. Regular check-ins:
   - Encourage your teen to review their calendar at the start and end of each week
   - Use this time to adjust deadlines if needed and plan for the week ahead
   - Celebrate met deadlines and problem-solve for any missed ones

Remember, the goal is to create a proactive approach to managing deadlines, reducing stress, and enhancing academic performance. Here are some additional tips to help your teen master deadline management:

1. Estimate realistically: Many teens underestimate how long tasks will take. Encourage your teen to track how long different types of assignments actually take them, so they can plan more accurately in the future.
2. Build in buffer time: Always plan to finish a day or two before the actual deadline. This allows for unexpected delays or last-minute revisions.
3. Break down larger projects: For big assignments, create a series of smaller deadlines leading up to the final due date.
4. Prioritize tasks: Use techniques like the Eisenhower Matrix to determine which tasks are urgent and important.
5. Communicate with teachers: If your teen is struggling to meet a deadline, encourage them to communicate with their

teacher early. Many teachers appreciate proactive communication and may be willing to grant extensions if asked in advance.

6. Learn from missed deadlines: If your teen does miss a deadline, treat it as a learning opportunity. Help them analyze what went wrong and how they can prevent it in the future.

By implementing these strategies, your teen can develop strong deadline management skills that will serve them well throughout their academic career and beyond.

Balancing School, Work, and Leisure

Finding the right balance between school, work, and leisure is crucial for your teen's overall well-being. It's about:

- Preventing burnout: Constant work without breaks leads to exhaustion and decreased productivity.
- Maintaining mental health: A balanced life helps manage stress and promotes emotional well-being.
- Enhancing productivity: Proper balance actually improves performance in all areas.
- Developing life skills: Learning to balance different aspects of life is a crucial skill for adulthood.
- Fostering personal growth: Time for hobbies and interests contributes to a well-rounded personality.

Here's how to create a balanced schedule:

1. Allocate time blocks for different activities:
   - Schoolwork: Include class time, homework, and study periods.
   - Extracurriculars: Sports practice, club meetings, volunteer work, etc.

- Personal interests: Hobbies, exercise, social time with friends.
- Family time: Meals together, family activities.
- Rest and self-care: Adequate sleep, relaxation time.

2. Prioritize tasks based on importance and urgency:
   - Use techniques like the Eisenhower Matrix to categorize tasks.
   - Ensure high-priority tasks get scheduled first.
   - Be realistic about what can be accomplished in a day.

3. Include downtime and relaxation in the schedule:
   - Schedule specific times for breaks and leisure activities.
   - Encourage activities that promote relaxation and stress relief.
   - Remember that downtime is not just "nice to have"—it's essential for mental health and productivity.

Setting boundaries is key:

- Limit work hours: Set a cut-off time for schoolwork each day.
- Designate study-free zones in the home: Create spaces where your teen can fully relax without thinking about work.
- Learn to say no to overcommitment: Help your teen understand that it's okay to decline some opportunities to maintain balance.
- Establish technology-free times: Implement periods where phones and computers are put away.

Remember to evaluate and adjust regularly. Conduct weekly reviews with your teen to assess how their schedule is working and make necessary adjustments. Ask questions like:

- Did you feel overly stressed or rushed this week?
- Were you able to complete all your important tasks?
- Did you have enough time for relaxation and fun?
- Is there anything you'd like to change for next week?

Here's a sample balanced daily schedule for a teen:

6:30 AM - Wake up, morning routine
7:30 AM - Breakfast and family time
8:00 AM - School
3:00 PM - After-school snack and short break
3:30 PM - Homework and studying
5:30 PM - Sports practice or hobby time
7:00 PM - Dinner and family time
8:00 PM - Free time (social media, TV, reading, etc.)
9:30 PM - Prepare for bed
10:00 PM - Lights out

Of course, this schedule would need to be adapted based on your teen's specific school hours, extracurricular commitments, and family routines. The key is to ensure there's a mix of productive time, social time, family time, and personal downtime each day.

Remember, balance doesn't mean every day has to be perfectly divided. Some days might be heavier on schoolwork, while others might have more time for leisure. The goal is to achieve balance over time, not necessarily within each day.

By helping your teen create and maintain a balanced schedule, you're teaching them valuable life skills and setting them up for long-term success and well-being.

Real-Life Case Study: Mastering Time Management

Meet Maya, a high school junior juggling academics, soccer, and a social life. Her grades were slipping, and stress levels were skyrocketing. Here's how she turned things around:

1. Implemented the Pomodoro Technique: Maya started using 30-minute work intervals followed by 10-minute breaks. This

helped her maintain focus during study sessions and prevented burnout.

2. Broke tasks into manageable steps: Large projects were divided into smaller, less daunting tasks with mini-deadlines. For instance, her history project was broken down into research, outlining, writing, and editing phases, each with its own deadline.

3. Created a balanced schedule: Time blocks were allocated for schoolwork, soccer practice, and relaxation. Maya used Google Calendar to color-code different activities and set reminders.

4. Tackled procrastination: Maya used the "Eat That Frog" technique, tackling challenging tasks first thing after school when her energy was highest.

5. Improved deadline management: She started using backward planning for long-term assignments, ensuring steady progress and avoiding last-minute rushes.

6. Set boundaries: Maya established a "no phone" rule during study times and communicated with friends about her new schedule to manage expectations.

7. Regular check-ins: Every Sunday evening, Maya reviewed her upcoming week with her parents, adjusting her schedule as needed.

The results?

- Improved grades: Maya's GPA increased from a 3.0 to a 3.7 over one semester.
- Reduced stress: She reported feeling more in control and less anxious about her workload.
- Better sleep: By managing her time more effectively, Maya was able to maintain a consistent sleep schedule.
- Improved athletic performance: With reduced academic stress, Maya found she had more energy for soccer practice.

- More quality leisure time: Efficient time management meant Maya could enjoy her free time without guilt or worry about unfinished tasks.

Challenges and adjustments:

- Initially, Maya struggled to stick to her Pomodoro intervals. She adjusted by starting with 20-minute work periods and gradually increasing to 30 minutes.
- She found that some tasks took longer than anticipated. Maya learned to build in buffer time when estimating task duration.
- There were times when social events conflicted with her study schedule. Maya learned to communicate with friends and sometimes say no to maintain balance.

Maya's story shows that with the right strategies and support, significant improvements in time management are possible. It's not about becoming a perfect time manager overnight, but about making consistent small improvements that add up to big changes.

As we wrap up this chapter, remember that mastering time management is a journey, not a destination. It takes practice, patience, and sometimes a bit of trial and error. But with these tools and strategies, your teen can learn to navigate their busy life with confidence and ease.

Encourage your teen to start small—perhaps by implementing just one or two of these strategies at first. As they see improvements, they'll likely be motivated to incorporate more techniques into their routine. And remember, what works for one teen might not work for another. The key is to find a personalized approach that fits your teen's unique needs and personality.

In the next chapter, we'll explore how emotional regulation and stress management play a vital role in supporting teens as they juggle their many responsibilities. Get ready to discover strategies that will help your teen stay calm and focused, even when life gets hectic!

FOUR

Emotional Regulation and Stress Management

Your teen bursts through the front door, slamming it behind them. Without a word, they storm up to their room, leaving a trail of tension in their wake. You've seen this before—the clenched jaw, the furrowed brow, the silence that speaks volumes. When you gently knock and enter their room, you find them buried under blankets, overwhelmed by the day's events.

Sound familiar? This scenario highlights a critical skill many teens struggle with: emotional regulation. It's not just about controlling outbursts; it's about navigating the complex world of feelings in a healthy, productive way. And in today's high-pressure world, it's more important than ever.

In this chapter, we'll dive into the world of emotional regulation and stress management. We'll explore practical strategies to help your teen handle their emotions, cope with stress, and build resilience. By the end, you'll have a toolkit to support your teen in developing these crucial life skills.

Understanding Emotional Regulation

Think of emotional regulation as your teen's internal thermostat. Just as a thermostat helps maintain a comfortable temperature in your home, emotional regulation helps your teen maintain a balanced emotional state. It's not about suppressing feelings, but rather managing and expressing them in healthy ways.

Why is this skill so crucial? Here's why:

1. Mental health: Good emotional regulation is linked to better mental health outcomes. Teens who can manage their emotions are less likely to experience anxiety and depression.
2. Relationship building: When teens can regulate their emotions, they're better equipped to navigate social situations and build strong relationships.
3. Improved problem-solving: Resilience helps teens approach problems with a can-do attitude, rather than feeling defeated.
4. Academic success: Emotional regulation helps teens focus on their studies, even when facing challenges or stress.
5. Future success: These skills lay the groundwork for success in college, careers, and adult relationships.

So, what exactly does emotional regulation involve? Let's break it down:

1. Emotional awareness: This is the ability to recognize and understand one's emotions. It's like being a detective of your own feelings, identifying what triggers certain emotions and how they manifest.
2. Impulse control: This involves the ability to pause before reacting to an emotional trigger. It's that moment of thought between feeling and action.

3. Emotional flexibility: This is the capacity to adapt emotional responses to different situations. It's about being able to shift gears emotionally when circumstances change.
4. Self-soothing techniques: These are methods to calm the mind and body during stressful or emotional times. Think deep breathing, visualization, or engaging in a calming activity.

Now, you might be wondering, "What's happening in my teen's brain during all this?" Great question! The brain plays a huge role in emotional regulation. Here's a simplified explanation:

- The amygdala: Think of this as the brain's emotional alarm system. It quickly reacts to perceived threats or intense emotions.
- The prefrontal cortex: This is like the brain's wise manager. It helps make decisions, control impulses, and regulate emotions.
- The limbic system: This includes the amygdala and other structures involved in emotional processing and memory formation.

During adolescence, these brain regions are still developing and fine-tuning their connections. This is why teens sometimes struggle with emotional regulation—their brain's "wise manager" is still learning on the job!

Understanding this brain activity can help you appreciate the challenges your teen faces in regulating their emotions. It's not just about willpower; it's about brain development too.

Here's a practical exercise to help your teen build emotional awareness:

Emotion Tracking Worksheet:

1. Emotion: Identify the emotion you're feeling.
2. Trigger: What caused this emotion?
3. Physical sensations: How does this emotion feel in your body?
4. Thoughts: What thoughts are associated with this emotion?
5. Reaction: How did you respond to this emotion?
6. Alternative response: Can you think of a different way to respond?

Encourage your teen to use this worksheet regularly. Over time, they'll start to see patterns in their emotional responses, which is the first step in improving emotional regulation.

Developing emotional regulation skills is a process. It takes time, practice, and patience. In the next section, we'll explore specific techniques for managing stress and anxiety—common challenges that go hand-in-hand with emotional regulation.

Techniques for Managing Stress and Anxiety

Let's face it: being a teen today is stressful. Between academic pressures, social dynamics, and the constant buzz of social media, it's no wonder many teens feel overwhelmed. But here's the good news: there are practical, effective strategies to manage stress and anxiety.

First, let's look at why stress management is so crucial:

1. Academic performance: Chronic stress can significantly impact a teen's ability to focus, learn, and perform well in school.

2. Physical health: Stress isn't just mental—it can manifest physically too. Headaches, stomachaches, and fatigue are common symptoms of stress in teens.
3. Social relationships: Stress can make teens irritable or withdrawn, straining their relationships with friends and family.
4. Long-term well-being: Learning to manage stress now sets the foundation for a healthier, happier adulthood.

So, what are the common sources of stress for teens? Here's a quick rundown:

- Academic pressures: The expectation to excel in school, get good grades, and prepare for college can be overwhelming.
- Social dynamics: Navigating friendships, dealing with peer pressure, and trying to fit in can be incredibly stressful.
- Family expectations: Pressure from parents to achieve or live up to certain standards can add to a teen's stress load.
- Extracurricular commitments: While beneficial, juggling sports, clubs, and other activities can sometimes feel like too much.

Now, let's dive into some practical strategies to help your teen manage stress and anxiety:

1. Promote a healthy lifestyle: This is the foundation of good stress management. Encourage your teen to:
   - Eat a balanced diet rich in fruits, vegetables, lean proteins, and whole grains.
   - Get 8-10 hours of sleep each night.
   - Stay hydrated by drinking plenty of water throughout the day.
   - Limit caffeine and sugar intake, which can exacerbate anxiety.

2. Teach relaxation techniques: These can be powerful tools for managing stress in the moment. Try:
    o Deep breathing exercises: Teach your teen to take slow, deep breaths when feeling stressed.
    o Progressive muscle relaxation: This involves tensing and then relaxing different muscle groups in the body.
    o Guided imagery: Using imagination to visualize a calm, peaceful place can be very soothing.
3. Encourage physical activity: Exercise is a great stress-buster. It releases endorphins, improves mood, and helps clear the mind. Help your teen find a physical activity they enjoy, whether it's team sports, yoga, dancing, or just taking regular walks.
    o Promote time management: Often, stress comes from feeling overwhelmed by tasks. Continue to reinforce the strategies covered in Chapter 3.
4. Foster a positive mindset: Help your teen reframe negative thoughts into more positive ones. For example, instead of "I'll never understand this math concept," encourage them to think, "This is challenging, but I can figure it out with practice."
5. Create a stress-relief toolkit: Work with your teen to assemble a collection of items that help them relax. This might include:
    o A favorite book or magazine
    o Stress balls or fidget toys
    o Calming music or nature sounds
    o A journal for writing out thoughts and feelings
    o Aromatherapy oils or candles with soothing scents
6. Limit technology use: While social media and smartphones can be fun, they can also be a source of stress. Encourage your teen to take regular breaks from technology and engage in face-to-face interactions or offline activities.

What works for one teen might not work for another. Encourage your teen to try different stress management techniques and find what works best for them. The goal is to build a personalized stress management toolkit they can rely on when things get tough.

Here's a simple exercise to help your teen identify their stress triggers and coping strategies:

Stress Management Worksheet:

1. Stressor: Identify a situation that causes stress.
2. Stress level: Rate the stress level from 1-10.
3. Physical reactions: How does your body respond to this stress?
4. Emotional reactions: What feelings come up?
5. Current coping strategy: How do you usually handle this stress?
6. Alternative strategies: List 3 new ways you could cope with this stress.
7. Action plan: Choose one new strategy to try next time you face this stressor.

By regularly using this worksheet, your teen can become more aware of their stress patterns and develop more effective coping strategies over time.

In the next section, we'll explore how to build emotional resilience—a key skill that helps teens bounce back from challenges and setbacks.

Building Emotional Resilience and Encouraging Positive Self-Talk

Think of emotional resilience as your teen's emotional shock absorbers. Just as shock absorbers help a car navigate bumpy roads, emotional resilience helps your teen navigate life's ups and downs. It's not about avoiding challenges, but about bouncing back from them stronger than before.

We know that emotional resilience promotes better mental health, improves problem solving, enhances relationships, and leads to greater academic success. So, how can we help our teens build this crucial skill? Here are some strategies:

1. Encourage a growth mindset: Teach your teen that abilities and intelligence can be developed through effort, learning, and persistence. This mindset helps them see challenges as opportunities for growth.
2. Foster problem-solving skills: When your teen faces a problem, resist the urge to solve it for them. Instead, guide them through the problem-solving process. Ask questions like, "What are your options?" or "What do you think might happen if you try this?"
3. Promote self-care: Help your teen develop habits that support their physical and emotional well-being. This might include regular exercise, getting enough sleep, or practicing mindfulness.
4. Build a support network: Encourage your teen to cultivate strong relationships with family, friends, and mentors. Having a support system can provide a safety net during tough times.
5. Teach stress management techniques: Equip your teen with tools to manage stress, such as deep breathing exercises, meditation, or journaling.
6. Encourage healthy risk-taking: Support your teen in stepping out of their comfort zone in safe ways. This could be trying a new hobby, speaking up in class, or joining a club.

A crucial component of building resilience is developing positive self-talk. The way we talk to ourselves has a profound impact on how we feel and behave. For many teens, negative self-talk can become a harmful habit, undermining their confidence and resilience.

Here are some strategies to help your teen develop more positive self-talk:

1. Identify negative self-talk: Help your teen become aware of their inner dialogue. Common forms of negative self-talk include:
   - All-or-nothing thinking: "If I don't get an A, I'm a total failure."
   - Overgeneralization: "I always mess things up."
   - Magnification: "This is the worst thing that could ever happen."
2. Challenge negative thoughts: Teach your teen to question their negative self-talk. Are these thoughts realistic? Is there evidence to support them?
3. Reframe negative statements: Help your teen transform negative self-talk into more positive, realistic statements. For example:
   - Instead of "I'm terrible at math," try "Math is challenging, but I can improve with practice."
   - Instead of "Nobody likes me," try "I have some good friends, and I can make more."
4. Use affirmations: Encourage your teen to create and use positive affirmations. These are short, powerful statements that can boost confidence and motivation. For example:
   - "I am capable of handling challenges."
   - "I learn from my mistakes and grow stronger."
   - "I am worthy of love and respect."
5. Practice gratitude: Regularly focusing on things to be thankful for can shift perspective and promote more positive thinking. Encourage your teen to keep a gratitude journal or share one thing they're grateful for each day.

Here's a practical exercise to help your teen transform negative self-talk:

Thought Transformation Worksheet:

1. Situation: Describe a challenging situation.
2. Negative thought: What negative thought came up?
3. Evidence for: What evidence supports this thought?
4. Evidence against: What evidence contradicts this thought?
5. Balanced thought: What's a more balanced, realistic way to think about this situation?
6. Positive affirmation: Create a positive statement to counteract the negative thought.

Changing thought patterns takes time and practice. Encourage your teen to be patient with themselves as they work on developing more positive self-talk.

Coping with Academic Pressure

In today's competitive academic environment, many teens feel overwhelmed by the pressure to excel. While some stress can be motivating, too much can be detrimental to both mental health and academic performance.

Here are some signs that your teen might be struggling with academic pressure:

1. Physical symptoms: Frequent headaches, stomach aches, or fatigue.
2. Sleep changes: Difficulty falling asleep, waking up frequently, or oversleeping.
3. Mood swings: Increased irritability, anxiety, or sadness.
4. Procrastination: Putting off schoolwork more than usual.

5. Perfectionism: Obsessing over grades or being overly self-critical.

6. Loss of interest: Withdrawing from activities they used to enjoy.

7. Declining grades: A sudden drop in academic performance.

If you notice these signs, it's important to address them promptly. Here are some strategies to help your teen manage academic pressure:

1. Teach time management: As we reviewed before, help your teen create a study schedule that allows for balance between schoolwork, extracurriculars, and relaxation. Use tools like planners or digital apps to keep track of assignments and deadlines.

2. Encourage breaks: Regular breaks during study sessions can actually improve focus and retention. The Pomodoro Technique (25 minutes of focused work followed by a 5-minute break) can be particularly effective.

3. Promote a growth mindset: Remind your teen that intelligence and abilities can be developed through effort and learning. This can help them see challenges as opportunities for growth rather than threats.

4. Set realistic goals: Help your teen set achievable academic goals. These should be challenging enough to motivate them, but not so difficult that they feel overwhelmed.

5. Prioritize self-care: Ensure your teen is getting enough sleep, eating well, and exercising regularly. These basic self-care practices can significantly impact both academic performance and stress levels.

6. Teach stress-reduction techniques: Deep breathing, meditation, or yoga can be powerful tools for managing academic stress.

7. Encourage seeking help: If your teen is struggling with a particular subject, encourage them to seek help from teachers, tutors, or study groups.

8. Maintain perspective: Remind your teen that while academics are important, they don't define a person's worth. Encourage them to view setbacks as learning opportunities rather than failures.

Here's a practical exercise to help your teen manage academic stress:

Academic Stress Management Plan:

1. Stressor: Identify a specific academic stressor (e.g., upcoming exam, difficult project).
2. Current feelings: How does this stressor make you feel?
3. Coping strategies: List three healthy ways you can cope with this stress.
4. Action steps: What specific steps can you take to address this stressor?
5. Support system: Who can you turn to for support or help?
6. Self-care plan: How will you take care of yourself while dealing with this stressor?

By regularly using this plan, your teen can develop a proactive approach to managing academic stress.

While it's important to encourage academic success, it's equally crucial to prioritize your teen's mental health and well-being. A balanced approach that values both achievement and emotional wellness will set your teen up for long-term success and happiness.

Developing a Growth Mindset

A growth mindset is the belief that abilities and intelligence can be developed through effort, learning, and persistence. This concept, developed by psychologist Carol Dweck, can be a game-changer for teens struggling with academic pressure and self-doubt.

Here's how a growth mindset differs from a fixed mindset:

Fixed Mindset:

- "I'm not good at math. I'll never understand it."
- "If I fail, it means I'm not smart enough."
- "Why try? I probably won't succeed anyway."

Growth Mindset:

- "Math is challenging, but I can improve with practice."
- "Failures are opportunities to learn and grow."
- "I can achieve my goals if I put in the effort and seek help when needed."

The benefits of a growth mindset are substantial:

1. Increased resilience: Teens with a growth mindset are more likely to persevere in the face of challenges.
2. Improved learning: They're more open to feedback and willing to put in effort to improve.
3. Greater achievement: Research shows that students with a growth mindset often outperform those with a fixed mindset.
4. Enhanced motivation: They're more likely to embrace challenges and stay motivated in the face of setbacks.

Here are some strategies to help your teen develop a growth mindset:

1. Praise effort, not just results: Instead of saying "You're so smart!", try "I'm proud of how hard you worked on that."
2. Encourage embracing challenges: Help your teen see difficult tasks as opportunities to grow, not threats to avoid.
3. Reframe failures: Teach your teen to view failures as learning experiences. Ask, "What can you learn from this?" rather than dwelling on the negative outcome.

4. Promote a love of learning: Encourage curiosity and exploration beyond just getting good grades.
5. Model a growth mindset yourself: Share your own experiences of overcoming challenges and learning new skills.
6. Use growth mindset language: Encourage phrases like "I can't do it yet" instead of "I can't do it."
7. Celebrate progress: Acknowledge improvements, no matter how small, to reinforce the value of effort and perseverance.

Here's a practical exercise to help your teen shift towards a growth mindset:

Mindset Shift Worksheet:

1. Fixed mindset thought: Write down a thought that reflects a fixed mindset.
2. Challenge: How does this thought limit you?
3. Evidence: What evidence do you have that this thought might not be true?
4. Growth mindset alternative: Rewrite the thought from a growth mindset perspective.
5. Action plan: What steps can you take to embrace this new perspective?

Real-Life Case Study: Thriving Under Pressure

Meet Olivia, a high school junior who initially struggled with emotional regulation and academic stress. She would get easily overwhelmed by her workload, leading to emotional outbursts and a sense of helplessness. Her parents, Megan and John, noticed these patterns and sought ways to support her.

They implemented several strategies:

1. Recognizing emotional triggers: They helped Olivia identify situations that caused her to feel overwhelmed.
2. Stress management techniques: Olivia began practicing mindfulness and engaging in regular physical activity.
3. Building emotional intelligence: She started journaling her feelings daily, gaining insights into her emotional patterns.
4. Developing a growth mindset: They encouraged Olivia to view challenges as opportunities for growth.

The journey wasn't without challenges. Olivia initially resisted some techniques, finding them tedious. Her parents adapted their approach, incorporating these practices into her daily routine in more engaging ways.

Over time, Olivia's emotional regulation skills improved significantly. She became more adept at recognizing and managing her triggers, reducing the frequency and intensity of her emotional outbursts. Her ability to handle stress and anxiety also improved, leading to better academic performance and healthier relationships.

Olivia's case highlights the transformative power of targeted strategies for emotional regulation and stress management. It underscores the importance of personalized approaches and the need for patience and flexibility in supporting teens through their emotional challenges.

As we conclude this chapter, remember that developing emotional regulation skills and managing stress is an ongoing process. It requires patience, practice, and support. By implementing these strategies and maintaining a supportive environment, you can help your teen build the resilience and emotional intelligence they need to thrive, not just in academics, but in all aspects of life.

Sharing the Power of Executive Functioning Skills

We have been exploring the critical role of executive functioning skills in teen development and discussing how these skills—including organization, time management, emotional regulation, and decision-making—have become increasingly crucial in our complex, fast-paced world. The digital age presents both challenges and opportunities for developing these skills, reshaping how teens learn, work, and interact with the world around them.

Building executive functioning skills isn't about imposing rigid structures or expecting perfection. It's about helping teens develop the tools they need to navigate their increasingly complex lives, understand their own thought processes, and develop the resilience to push through challenges and setbacks.

I hope that by this stage in your reading, you've seen how the strategies in this book can lead to positive outcomes such as improved academic performance, better stress management, and increased independence. If the insights and activities in this book have made a difference in your approach to supporting your teen's executive functioning development, then you're in the perfect position to help other parents and teens.

By leaving a review on Amazon, you'll help other readers discover the key steps they need to take to support their teens in developing crucial executive functioning skills.

Share your opinion of this book and a little bit about your own experiences applying its strategies. One of the most powerful ways to reinforce your own learning is to help others understand these important concepts.

Thank you for your support. Together, we can highlight the transformative power of understanding and nurturing teen executive functioning skills in our rapidly changing world.

Scan the QR code below to leave your review.

FIVE

Enhancing Focus and Attention

Your teen is sitting at the kitchen table, surrounded by textbooks, notebooks, and a laptop. But instead of diving into their homework, they're staring into space, fidgeting with their pen, or sneaking glances at their phone. Sound familiar?

In today's world of constant distractions, many teens struggle to maintain focus and attention. But don't worry - with the right strategies and understanding, you can help your teen sharpen their concentration skills and boost their productivity.

In this chapter, we'll explore the science behind focus, learn how to create an environment that supports concentration, and discover practical techniques for managing distractions. By the end, you'll have a toolkit to help your teen develop laser-like focus and attention.

Understanding the Science of Focus

Let's start by demystifying what's happening in your teen's brain when they're trying to focus. Think of the brain as a complex orchestra, with different sections working together to create beautiful music - or in this case, sustained attention.

The key players in this focus orchestra are:

1. The prefrontal cortex: This is like the conductor, coordinating all the other parts. It's responsible for decision-making, impulse control, and maintaining attention. When your teen is focusing on a task, their prefrontal cortex is working overtime to filter out distractions and keep them on track.
2. Dopamine: Think of this as the rhythm section, keeping everything moving. This neurotransmitter is crucial for motivation and focus. When dopamine levels are balanced, your teen feels motivated to start and complete tasks.
3. Neural pathways: These are like the sheet music, guiding the flow of information. The more your teen practices focusing, the stronger these pathways become. It's a classic case of "use it or lose it" - the more they exercise their focus muscles, the stronger they get.

Several factors can affect your teen's ability to focus:

- Environmental factors: A noisy or cluttered space can be like static interfering with the brain's focus signal. Just as it's hard to hear a quiet conversation in a noisy room, it's challenging for the brain to focus in a distracting environment.
- Emotional state: Stress or anxiety can drown out the focus orchestra, making it hard to concentrate. When your teen is worried about something, their brain is using energy to process those emotions, leaving less capacity for focusing on tasks.
- Nutrition: The brain needs the right fuel to function optimally. A balanced diet supports better focus. Think of it like putting premium gas in a high-performance car - the right nutrients can help your teen's brain run more efficiently.
- It's also important to be aware of attention disorders like ADHD (Attention-Deficit/Hyperactivity Disorder). If your teen consistently struggles with focus despite your best

efforts, it might be worth consulting a professional for an evaluation. ADHD is characterized by persistent patterns of inattention, hyperactivity, and impulsivity that interfere with daily functioning and development.

If you suspect your teen might have ADHD, it's crucial to seek a professional diagnosis. Treatment options can include behavioral therapy, medication, or a combination of both. Having ADHD doesn't mean your teen can't succeed - many people with ADHD lead successful, fulfilling lives. We'll dive into specific strategies for teens with ADHD in Chapter 8. The key is getting the right support and developing strategies to manage symptoms effectively.

Now, let's look at a practical exercise to help your teen tune into their focus patterns:

Focus Journal:

1. Tasks Completed: List what you managed to finish today.
2. Distractions: Note what pulled your attention away and how you dealt with it.
3. Emotional State: Reflect on your mood and how it affected your focus.
4. Diet and Exercise: Track what you ate and any physical activity.
5. Focus Rating: On a scale of 1-10, how would you rate your overall focus today?
6. Observations: Any patterns or insights you've noticed about your focus?

Encourage your teen to keep this journal for at least a week, then review it together. You might spot patterns that can help you develop targeted strategies for improving focus. For example, you might notice that your teen focuses better after physical activity, or that certain foods seem to boost their concentration.

Understanding the science of focus is the first step in helping your teen improve their concentration. By recognizing the factors that influence focus, you can work together to create an environment and routine that supports better attention and productivity.

Creating a Distraction-Free Environment

Now that we understand what's happening in the brain, let's look at how we can set the stage for better focus. The environment your teen studies in can make a huge difference in their ability to concentrate.

Imagine trying to read a book in the middle of a carnival - that's what it can feel like for your teen to study in a distracting environment. Here's how to create a focus-friendly space:

1. Organize the study space: A cluttered desk can lead to a cluttered mind. Help your teen clear their workspace, keeping only the essentials. This might mean investing in some organizational tools like desk organizers, file folders, or a bulletin board for important notes and reminders.
2. Optimize lighting: Good lighting reduces eye strain and helps maintain alertness. Natural light is best, but a good desk lamp works too. Avoid harsh fluorescent lights that can cause headaches and fatigue. Consider a lamp with adjustable brightness settings so your teen can customize the lighting to their needs.
3. Ensure comfort: An uncomfortable chair can be a constant distraction. Invest in an ergonomic chair if possible. The right chair should support good posture and be adjustable to fit your teen's body. Also, consider the height of the desk - your teen's feet should be flat on the floor and their arms should rest comfortably on the desk surface.
4. Minimize noise: Background noise can be a major focus-killer. Consider noise-canceling headphones or implementing "quiet hours" during study time. If your teen prefers some

background noise, try white noise or instrumental music designed to enhance focus.

5. Create tech-free zones: Designate certain areas of the house as no-phone zones to reduce digital distractions. This could be the study area, the dining room during meals, or the bedroom during sleep hours.

6. Control temperature: A room that's too hot or too cold can be distracting. Aim for a comfortable temperature, typically between 68-72°F (20-22°C).

7. Add some greenery: Studies have shown that plants can improve concentration and productivity. A small potted plant on the desk can make the space more inviting and potentially boost focus.

8. Personalize the space: While you want to minimize distractions, allowing your teen to add a few personal touches can make the space more inviting. This could be a favorite photo, an inspiring quote, or a small memento that motivates them.

Here's a detailed activity to get your teen involved in creating their ideal study space:

Distraction Audit and Action Plan:

1. List all potential distractions in the current study space.

2. Rate each distraction on a scale of 1-10 (1 being minor, 10 being major).

3. For each distraction rated 7 or above: a. Describe why it's distracting b. Brainstorm at least three potential solutions c. Choose the most feasible solution to implement

4. Create an action plan: a. What changes will be made? b. When will these changes be implemented? c. What resources (if any) are needed? d. How will you measure the effectiveness of these changes?

5. Implement the changes and track improvement in focus over two weeks.
6. After two weeks, reassess. What worked well? What needs further adjustment?

What works for one teen might not work for another. Encourage your teen to experiment and find what helps them focus best. Some teens might work well with complete silence, while others might prefer soft background music. Some might prefer a minimalist desk, while others might work better with more personal items around them.

It's also important to note that creating a distraction-free environment isn't a one-time task. It requires ongoing maintenance and adjustment. Encourage your teen to regularly declutter their workspace and reassess what's working and what isn't.

By involving your teen in the process of creating their ideal study environment, you're not only helping them improve their focus but also teaching them valuable skills in self-awareness and problem-solving. These skills will serve them well beyond their academic years, helping them create productive work environments throughout their lives.

Screen Time: Setting Healthy Boundaries

In our digital age, screens are often the biggest hurdle to maintaining focus. While technology can be a valuable tool for learning, unchecked screen time can lead to scattered attention and even digital addiction. The constant notifications, the lure of social media, and the endless entertainment options can make it incredibly difficult for teens to focus on their studies or other important tasks.

Here's why setting boundaries around screen time is crucial:

1. It ensures a balanced lifestyle, making room for other important activities like physical exercise, face-to-face social interactions, and creative pursuits.
2. It promotes better sleep, which is essential for focus and learning. The blue light emitted by screens can interfere with the body's natural sleep-wake cycle.
3. It reduces the constant temptation of digital distractions, allowing for longer periods of sustained focus.
4. It helps prevent digital addiction, which can have serious consequences for mental health and social development.
5. It encourages more mindful and intentional use of technology, rather than mindless scrolling or passive consumption.

So, how much screen time is appropriate? While there's no one-size-fits-all answer, experts generally recommend no more than two hours of recreational screen time per day for teens. This doesn't include time spent on screens for educational purposes or homework. However, it's important to note that even educational screen time should be balanced with offline activities.

Here are some detailed strategies to help manage screen time:

1. Create a family media plan: Set clear rules about when and where screens can be used. Involve your teen in creating this plan to increase buy-in. This plan should cover all family members, not just the teens, as it's important for parents to model healthy screen habits too.
2. Use screen time tracking apps: Apps like Screen Time (for iOS) or Digital Wellbeing (for Android) can help monitor and limit device usage. These apps can provide eye-opening data about how much time is spent on different apps and websites.
3. Establish tech-free zones and times: For example, no phones at the dinner table or in bedrooms after a certain hour. This

not only reduces screen time but also promotes better family communication and sleep hygiene.

4. Implement a 'parking lot' system: Create a designated spot where all family members park their devices during certain hours, like during family time or before bedtime.

5. Encourage alternative activities: Help your teen discover and engage in offline hobbies and activities they enjoy. This could be sports, art, reading, or spending time in nature.

6. Practice the 20-20-20 rule: For every 20 minutes spent looking at a screen, take a 20-second break to look at something 20 feet away. This can help reduce eye strain and provide mini-breaks from screen focus.

7. Model good habits: Remember, your teen is watching you. If you're constantly on your phone, they'll likely follow suit. Make a conscious effort to limit your own screen time and engage in offline activities.

Here's a more detailed template to help you create a family media plan:

Family Media Plan:

1. Screen-Free Zones: (e.g., dining room, bedrooms, car)
2. Screen-Free Times: (e.g., during meals, 1 hour before bedtime, first hour after waking up)
3. Daily Screen Time Limits: a. Weekdays: (e.g., 2 hours of recreational screen time) b. Weekends: (e.g., 3 hours of recreational screen time)
4. Content Guidelines: (What types of content are allowed/not allowed?)
5. Device Curfew: (When do all devices get turned off for the night?)
6. Social Media Rules: (e.g., which platforms are allowed, privacy settings)

1. Consequences for breaking rules: (Be specific and consistent)
2. Rewards for following rules: (Consider non-screen rewards)
3. Family Screen-Free Activities: (List activities you'll do together without screens)
4. Regular Check-ins: (Set a schedule to review and adjust the plan as needed)

By setting clear boundaries around screen time, you're helping your teen develop healthy digital habits that will serve them well into adulthood. Remember, the goal isn't to demonize technology, but to help your teen use it in a way that enhances rather than detracts from their life and focus.

Social Media Distractions: How to Minimize Their Impact

Social media can be particularly challenging when it comes to maintaining focus. The constant stream of notifications, the fear of missing out (FOMO), and the addictive nature of scrolling can all wreak havoc on your teen's attention span. It's important to understand how social media affects focus and what can be done to mitigate its negative impacts.

Here's a deeper look at how social media can impact focus:

1. It creates a cycle of distraction and procrastination: The urge to check social media can interrupt focus every few minutes, making it difficult to concentrate on any task for an extended period.
2. It can lead to comparison and negative emotions: Seeing curated highlights of others' lives can trigger feelings of inadequacy or anxiety, further disrupting focus and emotional well-being.
3. It encourages multitasking: Switching between social media and other tasks can give the illusion of productivity, but actually reduces overall efficiency and the quality of work.

4. It shortens attention span: The rapid-fire nature of social media content can make it harder to focus on longer, more complex tasks.
5. It can be addictive: The dopamine hit from likes and comments can create a cycle of seeking constant validation, making it harder to focus on less immediately rewarding tasks.

To help your teen manage social media distractions, consider these expanded strategies:

1. Set specific times for social media use: Encourage your teen to check social media during designated break times rather than constantly throughout the day. For example, they might allow themselves 15 minutes of social media time after completing an hour of focused work.
2. Use apps to limit access: Tools like Freedom, AppBlock, or built-in phone features can restrict access to social media during study times. Some of these apps allow you to set up recurring schedules, so social media is automatically blocked during designated study hours.
3. Encourage mindful use: Help your teen be more intentional about their social media interactions. Instead of mindless scrolling, they could set specific goals for their social media time, such as connecting with a certain number of friends or finding inspiration for a project.
4. Promote face-to-face interactions: Encourage your teen to connect with friends in person when possible. Real-life social interactions can be more fulfilling and less distracting than digital ones. This could involve joining clubs, participating in sports, or simply hanging out with friends.
5. Practice digital detox: Encourage periodic breaks from social media, such as a "social media-free weekend" once a month. This can help reset habits and reduce dependency on these platforms.

6. Curate the feed: Help your teen clean up their social media feeds by unfollowing or muting accounts that don't add value or that negatively impact their mood or focus.
7. Turn off notifications: Encourage your teen to disable push notifications for social media apps. This can significantly reduce the temptation to check constantly.
8. Use social media blocking extensions: For computer use, browser extensions like StayFocusd or Limit can block social media sites during designated work times.

Here's a reflective exercise to help your teen become more aware of their social media habits:

Social Media Audit and Action Plan:

1. Track social media use for a week: a. Time spent on each platform b. Purpose of each use (e.g., entertainment, communication, information) c. Mood before and after using social media
2. Reflect on the following questions: a. How do you feel when you can't access social media? b. How often do you check social media while doing other tasks? c. How does social media impact your sleep? d. Which social media interactions are most meaningful to you? e. Which ones leave you feeling drained or negative?
3. Identify patterns and areas for improvement: a. What are your most time-consuming platforms? b. When are you most likely to get distracted by social media? c. Which social media habits do you think are unhealthy?
4. Set goals for more mindful social media use: a. Specific times for checking social media b. Platforms you want to use less (or more) c. Types of content you want to engage with more
5. Create an action plan: a. List 3-5 specific changes you want to make b. How will you implement these changes? c. How will you measure success?

6. Implement your plan for two weeks, then reassess: a. What worked well? b. What was challenging? c. How do you feel after making these changes? d. What further adjustments do you want to make?

The goal isn't to eliminate social media entirely, but to help your teen use it in a way that enhances rather than detracts from their life and focus. By becoming more aware of their habits and intentional about their use, teens can learn to harness the benefits of social media while minimizing its potential for distraction.

The Role of Nutrition and Sleep in Focus

You've probably heard the phrase "you are what you eat." When it comes to focus, this couldn't be more true. What your teen puts into their body can have a significant impact on their ability to concentrate. Similarly, the quantity and quality of sleep they get plays a crucial role in their cognitive function and ability to focus.

Let's dive deeper into the nutritional aspect first:

Here are some focus-friendly foods to incorporate into your teen's diet:

1. Nuts and seeds: Packed with omega-3 fatty acids and vitamin E. Walnuts, in particular, are excellent for brain health.
2. Leafy greens: High in folate and vitamins that support cognitive function. Spinach, kale, and collard greens are great options.
3. Whole grains: Provide a steady supply of energy to the brain. They help maintain mental alertness throughout the day.
4. Lean proteins: Help produce neurotransmitters essential for focus. Fish, poultry, and legumes are excellent sources.
5. Eggs: Rich in choline, which is crucial for memory and mental function.

6. Dark chocolate: Contains caffeine and antioxidants that can enhance focus and concentration. Opt for varieties with at least 70% cocoa content.
7. Avocados: High in monounsaturated fats that support brain function and improve blood flow to the brain.
8. Berries: All berries are rich in antioxidants that can improve memory and cognitive function.
9. Green tea: Contains L-theanine, an amino acid that can help improve focus and attention.

Foods to avoid or limit include:

- Sugary snacks and drinks: These can cause energy crashes and negatively impact concentration.
- Highly processed foods: Often lack the nutrients needed for optimal brain function.
- Excessive caffeine: While small amounts can boost focus, too much can lead to jitters and difficulty concentrating.

Now, let's talk about sleep. Just as important as what your teen eats is how much they sleep. Adequate sleep is crucial for focus, memory consolidation, and overall cognitive function. Teens need about 8-10 hours of sleep per night.

Here's why sleep is so important for focus:

1. Memory consolidation: During sleep, the brain processes and stores information learned during the day.
2. Attention restoration: Sleep helps reset the brain's ability to focus and pay attention.
3. Emotional regulation: Lack of sleep can lead to mood swings and irritability, which can interfere with focus.
4. Cognitive performance: Well-rested teens perform better on tasks requiring attention and decision-making.

To promote better sleep:

1. Establish a consistent sleep schedule, even on weekends. This helps regulate the body's internal clock.
2. Create a relaxing bedtime routine. This might include reading a book, taking a warm bath, or practicing gentle stretches.
3. Limit screen time before bed. The blue light emitted by screens can interfere with the production of melatonin, a hormone that regulates sleep.
4. Ensure the bedroom is dark, quiet, and cool. These conditions are optimal for quality sleep.
5. Avoid caffeine in the afternoon and evening, as it can interfere with falling asleep.
6. Encourage regular exercise, but not too close to bedtime. Physical activity can improve sleep quality when done earlier in the day.
7. Consider using a white noise machine or app to create a consistent, soothing background noise.

Here's an expanded version of the sleep and nutrition tracker your teen can use:

Daily Wellness Log:

1. Hours of sleep:
2. Quality of sleep (1-10):
3. Meals and snacks (be specific):
   ◦ Breakfast:
   ◦ Lunch:
   ◦ Dinner:
   ◦ Snacks:
4. Water intake (glasses or ounces):
5. Caffeine intake (type and amount):
6. Physical activity (type and duration):
7. Energy level throughout the day (1-10):

- ◦ Morning:
- ◦ Afternoon:
- ◦ Evening:
8. Focus level throughout the day (1-10):
   - ◦ Morning:
   - ◦ Afternoon:
   - ◦ Evening:
9. Mood (describe):
10. Notable factors affecting sleep or focus:

Encourage your teen to keep this log for at least two weeks. You might notice patterns between their diet, sleep, and ability to focus. For instance, you might find that your teen focuses better after a protein-rich breakfast, or that they struggle to concentrate when they've had less than 8 hours of sleep.

Good nutrition and adequate sleep are foundational to cognitive function and focus. By helping your teen optimize these areas, you're setting them up for success not just in their studies, but in all areas of life.

Real-Life Case Study: Achieving Laser Focus

Meet Alex, a high school junior struggling with focus and falling grades. Despite being bright, Alex was easily distracted, disorganized, and spent too much time on his phone and social media.

When I first met Alex, his parents voiced concerns about his inability to stay focused. His room was a mess, his study habits were inconsistent, and he often seemed overwhelmed by his workload. It was clear that Alex needed a structured plan to regain his focus and improve his academic performance.

Here's how we helped Alex improve his focus:

1. Created a distraction-free study space: We started by decluttering Alex's desk, ensuring that only essential study materials remained. We added proper lighting with an adjustable desk lamp and invested in a comfortable, ergonomic chair. This clean, organized environment helped Alex feel more in control and less overwhelmed by his tasks.

2. Implemented screen time limits: We used tracking apps to monitor and limit Alex's device usage, especially during study hours. We set up specific times for checking social media and messages, rather than allowing constant access.

3. Established a consistent routine: We created a daily schedule that included dedicated study times, breaks, and a consistent sleep schedule. This routine helped Alex's brain know when it was time to focus on work and when it was time to relax.

4. Improved nutrition: We worked with Alex to incorporate more brain-boosting foods into his diet and reduce sugary snacks. We introduced foods like blueberries, nuts, and leafy greens, and encouraged him to stay hydrated throughout the day.

5. Enhanced sleep habits: We established a bedtime routine that included turning off screens an hour before bed and creating a cool, dark sleeping environment. This helped Alex get the 8-9 hours of sleep he needed to stay focused during the day.

6. Introduced mindfulness techniques: We taught Alex simple meditation and deep breathing exercises to help him refocus when distracted. These techniques proved particularly useful during study sessions and before exams.

7. Broke tasks into manageable chunks: We used the Pomodoro Technique, breaking study sessions into 25-minute focused work periods followed by 5-minute breaks. This helped prevent burnout and maintained Alex's motivation.

The journey wasn't always smooth. Alex initially resisted the changes, especially the limits on his phone use. We adjusted by allowing short, scheduled breaks for checking messages. We also introduced non-screen activities during these breaks, like quick stretches or walks.

Another challenge was maintaining consistency with the new habits. To address this, we created a reward system. For every week Alex stuck to his routine, he earned points that could be exchanged for privileges like extra weekend screen time or a favorite meal.

We also faced setbacks when Alex's motivation dipped after a particularly challenging exam. We used this as an opportunity to revisit his goals and remind him of the progress he'd made. We adjusted his study techniques for that subject, incorporating more visual aids and practice problems.

Over time, the results were remarkable. Alex's focus improved, his grades went up, and he felt more in control of his life. His parents observed that he was less stressed and more engaged in family activities. Alex's teachers also noticed the change, reporting that he was more attentive in class and submitting higher quality work.

Perhaps most importantly, Alex developed a sense of confidence in his ability to manage his time and focus. He started taking on leadership roles in group projects and even began mentoring younger students on study skills.

Reflecting on the journey, Alex shared, "At first, I thought all these changes would be restrictive and no fun. But actually, I feel so much more free now. I get my work done faster and better, and I enjoy my free time without feeling guilty about unfinished assignments."

Alex's parents expressed immense gratitude for the transformation they witnessed. His mother noted, "It's not just about the grades. We've seen Alex grow into a more responsible, confident young man. He's learning skills that will serve him well beyond high school."

Alex's story highlights several key points:

1. The importance of a holistic approach: Improving focus isn't just about willpower. It involves creating the right environment, managing technology use, maintaining good nutrition and sleep habits, and learning techniques to manage attention.
2. The value of consistency and routine: Regular habits help train the brain to focus at the right times.
3. The need for flexibility: What works for one person might not work for another. It's important to be willing to adjust strategies as needed.
4. The power of small changes: Each individual change might seem small, but together they created a significant impact on Alex's life.
5. The long-term benefits: The skills Alex learned didn't just improve his grades; they set him up for success in college and beyond.

This case study demonstrates that with the right strategies and support, any teen can improve their focus and attention. It takes time, consistency, and sometimes trial and error, but the payoff in improved performance and reduced stress is well worth the effort.

As we wrap up this chapter, remember that enhancing focus is an ongoing process. Encourage your teen to keep experimenting with these strategies to find what works best for them. With practice, they'll develop the ability to concentrate deeply - a skill that will serve them well through life.

In the next chapter, we'll explore how to set goals, prioritize tasks, and make effective decisions. These skills build on the foundation of focus we've established here, helping your teen channel their newfound concentration into achieving their dreams.

Goal Setting, Prioritization, and Decision Making

Your teen is staring at a mountain of homework, extracurricular commitments, and personal goals. They're overwhelmed, unsure where to start, and feeling like they're drowning in responsibilities. Sound familiar?

Don't worry - you're not alone. Many teens struggle with setting goals, prioritizing tasks, and making decisions. But with the right strategies and support, your teen can transform from feeling overwhelmed to feeling empowered and in control.

In this chapter, we'll explore powerful techniques for goal setting, task prioritization, and effective decision-making. By the end, you'll have a toolkit to help your teen navigate their responsibilities with confidence and purpose.

The Importance of Setting SMART Goals

Let's start with a game-changer: SMART goals. This isn't just another acronym - it's a powerful framework that can revolutionize how your teen approaches their objectives.

SMART stands for: **S**pecific, **M**easurable, **A**chievable, **R**elevant, **T**ime-bound

Here's why each element matters:

1. Specific: Vague goals lead to vague results. A specific goal answers the who, what, why, and where. Instead of "I want to do better in school," a specific goal might be "I want to improve my math grade."
2. Measurable: If you can't measure it, you can't manage it. Measurable goals allow your teen to track their progress. "I want to improve my math grade from a B to an A" is measurable and provides a clear target.
3. Achievable: Goals should stretch your teen's abilities but still be within reach. "Study math for one hour daily" is achievable if it fits into their schedule. Unrealistic goals lead to frustration, while achievable ones foster a sense of accomplishment.
4. Relevant: Goals should align with your teen's interests and long-term objectives. Improving a math grade is relevant if it supports their dream of becoming an engineer, for example.
5. Time-bound: Deadlines create urgency and help your teen stay focused. "I want to improve my math grade by the end of the semester" provides a clear timeframe for action.

The benefits of SMART goals are numerous:

- They provide clarity, reducing confusion and helping your teen focus their efforts.
- They increase motivation by allowing your teen to see clear, measurable progress.
- They enable better tracking, making it easier to adjust strategies if needed.

Let's look at some examples of well-defined SMART goals:

Academic goal: "Improve my math grade from a B to an A by the end of the semester by studying for one hour daily and attending weekly tutoring sessions."

Personal goal: "Run a 5K race in three months by following a weekly training plan and gradually increasing my running distance."

Here's how you can help your teen create their own SMART goals:

1. Start by identifying areas for improvement. Have an open discussion about what your teen wants to achieve and why it matters to them.
2. Help them make their goals specific and measurable. Ask questions like "How will you know when you've achieved this goal?"
3. Ensure the goals are achievable. Consider your teen's current abilities and resources. The goal should be challenging but not impossible.
4. Check that the goals are relevant to your teen's interests and long-term aspirations. This alignment keeps them engaged and motivated.
5. Set clear timelines. Break down larger goals into smaller, time-bound milestones.

Remember, goal-setting is a skill that improves with practice. Encourage your teen to regularly review and adjust their goals, celebrating progress along the way.

Here's a practical exercise to get started:

SMART Goal Workshop:

1. Choose one academic and one personal goal.
2. Use the SMART framework to refine each goal.
3. Write down the goals and the steps needed to achieve them.

4. Create a timeline for each goal, including milestones.
5. Schedule regular check-ins to review progress and make adjustments.

By guiding your teen through this process, you're equipping them with a powerful tool for achieving success. SMART goals provide a clear roadmap, keeping them focused, motivated, and on track to reach their full potential.

In the next section, we'll explore how to prioritize tasks effectively, ensuring your teen can manage their time and energy efficiently as they work towards their goals.

Prioritizing Tasks Effectively

Now that your teen has set SMART goals, the next challenge is managing the day-to-day tasks that will lead them to success. This is where prioritization comes in.

Imagine your teen's to-do list as a jumbled puzzle. Prioritization is the process of sorting those pieces, figuring out which ones are crucial and which can wait. It's about making smart choices with limited time and energy.

Why is prioritization so important? Here's why:

1. It prevents overwhelm: A long, unorganized list of tasks can be paralyzing. Prioritization breaks it down into manageable chunks.
2. It boosts productivity: By focusing on what's truly important, your teen can make significant progress on their goals.
3. It reduces stress: Knowing what needs to be done and when can alleviate anxiety about missed deadlines or forgotten tasks.
4. It helps with time management: Prioritization ensures that time is spent on high-impact activities rather than busy work.

Let's explore some effective prioritization strategies:

The Eisenhower Matrix

This powerful tool, named after President Dwight D. Eisenhower, helps categorize tasks based on their urgency and importance. Here's how it works:

1. Urgent and Important: Do these tasks immediately. Examples: Finishing a project due tomorrow, studying for a test next morning.
2. Important but Not Urgent: Schedule these for later. Examples: Long-term project planning, regular study sessions.
3. Urgent but Not Important: Delegate if possible. Examples: Some emails, certain meetings.
4. Neither Urgent nor Important: Eliminate these. Examples: Excessive social media scrolling, binge-watching TV shows.

Encourage your teen to use this matrix when planning their week or day. It can be eye-opening to see where their time is really going.

Creating Daily Task Lists

Help your teen start each day with a prioritized task list. Here's a simple method:

1. List all tasks for the day.
2. Categorize each task as high, medium, or low priority.
3. Assign specific time slots to high-priority tasks.
4. Fit medium-priority tasks around these.
5. Low-priority tasks get done if there's time left over.

Remember, flexibility is key. New tasks may arise, and priorities might shift. Teach your teen to reassess their list throughout the day and adjust as needed.

Here's a practical exercise to help your teen get started with prioritization:

Task Prioritization Workshop:

1. List all tasks and commitments for the coming week.
2. Use the Eisenhower Matrix to categorize each task.
3. Create a daily schedule, allocating time for high-priority tasks first.
4. Identify tasks that can be delegated or eliminated.
5. At the end of each day, review and adjust the next day's plan.

By mastering prioritization, your teen will learn to focus on what truly matters, making steady progress towards their goals while managing their daily responsibilities effectively.

Using Visual Aids to Track Progress

Now that your teen has set SMART goals and learned to prioritize tasks, it's time to talk about tracking progress. This is where visual aids come in handy.

Why are visual aids so powerful? Because they provide a tangible representation of progress. They're like a map, showing your teen how far they've come and how far they have left to go. This visual feedback can be incredibly motivating, especially when the journey towards a goal feels long or challenging.

Let's explore some effective visual aids:

Progress Charts

These are simple yet powerful tools. A progress chart could be a bar graph showing grades over time, or a line chart tracking study hours. The key is to make it visually appealing and easy to update.

For example, if your teen's goal is to improve their math grade, they could create a chart with test scores on the y-axis and dates on the x-axis. Each new test score gets plotted, creating a visual representation of their progress.

Vision Boards

A vision board is a collage of images and words that represent your teen's goals and aspirations. It's a creative way to keep goals front and center.

To create a vision board:

1. Gather magazines, printouts, photos, and inspirational quotes.
2. Choose a large poster board or cork board.
3. Have your teen select images and words that represent their goals.
4. Arrange and glue these elements onto the board.
5. Display the board where your teen will see it daily.

Task Boards

Inspired by project management techniques, task boards help visualize workflow. They typically have columns like "To Do," "In Progress," and "Done."

Your teen can create a task board using a whiteboard, bulletin board, or even a digital tool like Trello. As tasks move from left to right, your teen gets a visual sense of progress and accomplishment.

Digital Tools

In our tech-savvy world, don't overlook digital tools for tracking progress. Apps like Habitica turn goal-tracking into a game, while tools like Google Calendar can help visualize how time is spent.

Here's a fun activity to get your teen started with visual aids:

Progress Tracking Art Project:

1. Choose a goal to track visually.
2. Decide on a visual representation (chart, board, digital tool, etc.).
3. Gather necessary materials.
4. Create the visual aid together, making it colorful and personalized.
5. Determine how and when progress will be updated.
6. Display the visual aid prominently.

Remember, the best visual aid is one that resonates with your teen. Encourage them to get creative and find a method that feels inspiring and fun to use.

By incorporating visual aids into their goal-tracking process, your teen can stay motivated, celebrate progress, and maintain focus on their objectives. It's a powerful way to turn abstract goals into concrete, visible achievements.

Balancing Short-Term and Long-Term Goals

Imagine your teen is juggling several balls - some represent immediate tasks, others represent future aspirations. The trick is to keep all of these balls in the air without dropping any. This is the essence of balancing short-term and long-term goals.

Short-term goals are the stepping stones that lead to long-term success. They're the daily and weekly tasks that, when accomplished consistently, pave the way to bigger achievements. Long-term goals, on the other hand, are the big picture aspirations that give direction and purpose to these daily efforts.

Here's why understanding this balance is crucial:

1. It provides motivation: Short-term goals offer quick wins that keep your teen motivated, while long-term goals provide the overarching purpose.
2. It develops time management skills: Balancing both types of goals teaches your teen to manage their time effectively across different timescales.
3. It builds resilience: Working towards long-term goals while managing short-term tasks develops perseverance and adaptability.
4. It enhances decision-making: Understanding how short-term actions impact long-term outcomes improves your teen's ability to make wise choices.

Let's look at some strategies for creating this balance:

Setting Milestones

Milestones are like checkpoints on the road to a long-term goal. They break down the journey into manageable segments. For example, if your teen's long-term goal is to get into a prestigious university, milestones might include:

- Achieving a certain GPA each semester
- Scoring target points on standardized tests
- Completing a certain number of community service hours
- Securing leadership positions in extracurricular activities

By focusing on these milestones, your teen can see tangible progress towards their long-term goal while managing short-term tasks.

Aligning Daily Actions with Long-Term Vision

Help your teen see how their daily activities contribute to their long-term goals. For instance:

- Daily math practice (short-term) supports the goal of improving their math grade (medium-term), which contributes to their dream of becoming an engineer (long-term).
- Weekly soccer practice (short-term) builds skills for winning matches (medium-term), potentially leading to a college sports scholarship (long-term).

This alignment gives purpose to daily tasks and keeps your teen motivated even when the work gets challenging.

Regular Review and Adjustment

Goals aren't set in stone. Life changes, new opportunities arise, and priorities shift. Encourage your teen to regularly review and adjust their goals. Here's a simple process:

1. Monthly Check-in: Review progress on short-term goals and how they're contributing to long-term objectives.
2. Quarterly Assessment: Evaluate overall progress, celebrate achievements, and identify areas for improvement.
3. Annual Review: Reassess long-term goals, set new short-term objectives, and make any necessary adjustments to the overall plan.

This flexibility ensures that your teen's goals remain relevant and achievable as they grow and change.

Here's a practical exercise to help your teen balance their goals:

Goal Balancing Workshop:

1. List all current short-term and long-term goals.
2. For each long-term goal, identify 3-5 short-term actions that support it.
3. Create a timeline that includes both short-term tasks and long-term milestones.
4. Discuss how daily and weekly activities align with long-term aspirations.
5. Schedule monthly, quarterly, and annual review sessions.

By mastering this balance, your teen will develop a strategic mindset that serves them well in school, future careers, and life in general.

Staying Motivated and Overcoming Setbacks

The path to achieving goals is rarely a straight line. There will be ups and downs, moments of triumph and times of frustration. The key to success lies in staying motivated through it all and bouncing back from setbacks.

Why is motivation so crucial? It's the fuel that keeps your teen moving towards their goals, even when the going gets tough. It's what gets them out of bed to study, practice, or work on their projects. Without motivation, even the best-laid plans can fall apart.

Let's explore some strategies to keep that motivational fire burning:

Celebrate Small Wins

Every step forward, no matter how small, is progress. Encourage your teen to celebrate these small victories:

- Completing a challenging homework assignment
- Sticking to a study schedule for a week
- Improving a test score, even if it's just by a few points

These celebrations reinforce positive behaviors and provide a motivational boost.

Visualize Success

Visualization is a powerful tool used by athletes, entrepreneurs, and high achievers in every field. Encourage your teen to spend a few minutes each day visualizing themselves achieving their goals:

- What does success look like?
- How does it feel?
- What steps did they take to get there?

This mental rehearsal can boost confidence and motivation.

Use a Motivation Journal

A motivation journal can be a powerful tool for maintaining focus and enthusiasm. Encourage your teen to write in their journal daily, addressing prompts like:

- What are you grateful for today?
- What progress did you make towards your goals?
- What challenges did you overcome?
- What are you looking forward to tomorrow?

This practice keeps goals front and center and helps maintain a positive mindset.

Create a Support Network

Surrounding yourself with supportive people can make a huge difference in staying motivated. Encourage your teen to:

- Share their goals with friends and family who will cheer them on
- Find a study buddy or accountability partner
- Join clubs or groups related to their interests and goals

Having people to share the journey with can provide encouragement, advice, and motivation.

Now, let's talk about overcoming setbacks. Setbacks are a normal part of any journey towards a goal. The key is not to avoid them (which is impossible) but to learn how to bounce back from them. Here are some strategies:

Reframe Failures as Learning Opportunities

Help your teen see setbacks not as failures, but as valuable lessons. Ask questions like:

- What can you learn from this experience?
- How can you use this knowledge to improve next time?
- What would you do differently if you could do it over?

This reframing turns negative experiences into stepping stones for growth.

Adjust Goals Without Giving Up

Sometimes, setbacks mean it's time to adjust goals. This isn't giving up - it's being flexible and realistic. If your teen is struggling to meet a goal, help them:

- Break it down into smaller, more manageable steps
- Extend the timeline if needed
- Modify the goal to better fit their current circumstances

Remember, the aim is progress, not perfection.

Seek Inspiration from Others

Share stories of famous people who overcame setbacks on their path to success. For example: Michael Jordan was cut from his high school basketball team before becoming one of the greatest players of all time.

These stories remind us that setbacks are a normal part of any success story.

Here's a practical exercise to help your teen build resilience and stay motivated:

Motivation and Resilience Toolkit:

1. Create a "Wins" jar: Write down small victories on slips of paper and add them to the jar. Review these during tough times for a motivation boost.
2. Design a vision board representing goals and aspirations.
3. Start a motivation journal with daily prompts.
4. List 5 people who can provide support and encouragement.
5. Write a letter to your future self, describing your goals and the steps you're taking to achieve them.
6. Create a "Lessons Learned" document to record insights from setbacks.

By implementing these strategies, your teen can maintain motivation, bounce back from setbacks, and stay on track towards their goals. Remember, it's not about avoiding challenges - it's about developing the resilience to overcome them.

Real-Life Case Study: From Goals to Achievements

Let's meet Clara, a high school sophomore with big dreams but struggling to turn them into reality. Clara wanted to attend a top-tier university, but she often felt overwhelmed by her responsibilities. Her grades were good, but not great, and she struggled to balance her academic work with extracurricular activities and personal interests.

Clara's parents noticed her frustration and decided to help her implement the strategies we've discussed in this chapter. Here's how Clara's journey unfolded:

Setting SMART Goals

Clara and her parents sat down to set SMART goals. Instead of the vague "do better in school," they crafted specific, measurable goals:

1. "Raise my historygrade from a B to an A by the end of the semester by studying for 1 hour daily and attending weekly tutoring sessions."
2. "Join two extracurricular activities and take on a leadership role in at least one by the end of the school year."

These goals gave Clara clear targets to aim for and a roadmap to follow.

Prioritizing Tasks

Clara learned to use the Eisenhower Matrix to prioritize her tasks. She realized she was spending too much time on urgent but unimportant tasks, like responding to every social media notification. By focusing on important tasks first, she found she had more time and energy for what really mattered.

She created a daily task list, categorizing tasks as high, medium, or low priority. This helped her focus on what was truly important each day.

Using Visual Aids

Clara created a vision board with images of her dream university, inspirational quotes, and pictures representing her goals. She hung this in her room where she could see it every day.

She also started using a task board to track her progress on assignments and projects. Moving tasks from "To Do" to "Done" gave her a sense of accomplishment and motivation.

Balancing Short-Term and Long-Term Goals

Clara learned to see how her daily actions contributed to her long-term goals. She set milestones for her long-term goal of attending a top university:

- Achieve a 3.8 GPA by the end of sophomore year
- Score 1400+ on the PSAT by junior year
- Complete 100 hours of community service by senior year

These milestones helped her stay focused on her long-term vision while managing her day-to-day responsibilities.

Staying Motivated and Overcoming Setbacks

Clara faced challenges along the way. She struggled with her first few history tests, despite her increased study time. Instead of giving up, she reframed this setback as a learning opportunity. She analyzed her mistakes, sought extra help from her teacher, and adjusted her study strategies.

To stay motivated, Clara started a "Wins" jar, writing down small victories and reading them when she needed a boost. She also found an accountability partner in her best friend, who shared similar academic goals.

The Outcome

Over the course of the school year, Clara's efforts paid off:

1. She raised her historygrade to an A and improved her overall GPA to 3.7.
2. She joined the debate club and the school newspaper, eventually becoming the editor of the paper.
3. She developed better time management skills, reducing her stress and enjoying her activities more.
4. She felt more confident and in control of her future, with a clear plan for achieving her goals.

Clara's parents noticed a significant change in her attitude. She was more focused, motivated, and proactive about her responsibilities. Clara herself felt a sense of empowerment, knowing she had the tools to tackle challenges and achieve her dreams.

Key Takeaways from Clara's Story

1. SMART goals provide clarity and direction, making big dreams feel achievable.
2. Prioritization helps manage time and energy effectively, focusing on what truly matters.
3. Visual aids serve as constant reminders and motivators, keeping goals at the forefront.
4. Balancing short-term and long-term goals ensures steady progress towards big aspirations.
5. Setbacks are not failures, but opportunities for learning and growth.

6. Consistent effort, coupled with the right strategies, leads to significant improvements over time.

Clara's journey demonstrates that with the right tools and mindset, any teen can transform their goals into achievements. It takes time, effort, and persistence, but the results are worth it.

As we wrap up this chapter, remember that goal-setting, prioritization, and decision-making are skills that improve with practice. Encourage your teen to keep refining these skills, adjusting their strategies as needed, and celebrating their progress along the way.

In the next chapter, we'll explore the crucial topic of parent-teen collaboration. We'll discuss how to communicate effectively with your teen, build trust, and work together towards their goals. This partnership is key to supporting your teen's growth and success, so get ready for some powerful insights and strategies!

SEVEN

Parent-Teen Collaboration

You come home after a long day, eager to connect with your teen. But instead of a warm greeting, you're met with a closed bedroom door and the muffled sound of music. When you finally do see your teen, your attempts at conversation are met with shrugs or one-word answers. Sound familiar?

The teenage years can be a challenging time for both parents and teens. As your child seeks independence, communication can break down, and conflicts can arise. But don't worry - with the right strategies and approach, you can strengthen your bond and navigate these years together successfully.

In this chapter, we'll explore effective communication techniques, collaborative planning strategies, and ways to build trust and accountability. By the end, you'll have a toolkit to help you and your teen work together more effectively, fostering a strong and supportive relationship.

Effective Communication Techniques

At the heart of any strong relationship is good communication. When it comes to teens, this becomes even more crucial. Here are some key techniques to enhance your communication with your teen:

Active Listening

Active listening is about truly hearing and understanding what your teen is saying, rather than just waiting for your turn to speak. Here's how to practice active listening:

1. Give your full attention: Put away your phone, turn off the TV, and focus entirely on your teen.
2. Show you're listening: Use nonverbal cues like nodding and maintaining eye contact to show you're engaged.
3. Reflect back what you hear: Paraphrase what your teen has said to ensure you've understood correctly. For example, "So you're feeling stressed about the upcoming exams?"
4. Avoid interrupting: Let your teen finish their thoughts before responding.
5. Ask clarifying questions: If something isn't clear, ask for more information rather than making assumptions.

The goal is to understand your teen's perspective, not to judge or solve their problems immediately.

Open-Ended Questions

Open-ended questions encourage deeper conversations and help your teen express themselves more fully. Instead of questions that can be answered with a simple "yes" or "no," try questions that invite more detailed responses:

Instead of: "Did you have a good day?" Try: "What was the best part of your day?"

Instead of: "Are you worried about the test?" Try: "How are you feeling about the upcoming test?"

These types of questions show your teen that you're genuinely interested in their thoughts and experiences.

Non-Verbal Communication

Your body language and tone of voice can speak volumes. Pay attention to these non-verbal cues:

1. Body posture: Keep an open posture (uncrossed arms, facing your teen) to show you're receptive to conversation.
2. Eye contact: Maintain appropriate eye contact to show you're engaged, but don't stare, which can feel intimidating.
3. Facial expressions: Be aware of your facial expressions. A furrowed brow might communicate disapproval when you're actually just concentrating.
4. Tone of voice: Keep your tone calm and neutral, even if the conversation becomes heated.

Empathy and Validation

Showing empathy and validating your teen's feelings is crucial for building trust and encouraging open communication. Here's how:

1. Acknowledge their feelings: Use phrases like "I can see why you'd feel that way" or "That sounds really tough."
2. Avoid dismissing their emotions: Steer clear of phrases like "It's not a big deal" or "You're overreacting."
3. Share similar experiences: If appropriate, share times when you've felt similarly. This can help your teen feel understood and less alone.

4. Offer support: Ask how you can help or simply be there to listen.

Here's a practical exercise to improve your communication skills:

Communication Check-In:

1. For one week, pay close attention to your communication with your teen.
2. After each significant conversation, reflect on these questions:
   - Did I practice active listening?
   - Did I use open-ended questions?
   - Was I aware of my non-verbal communication?
   - Did I show empathy and validate their feelings?
3. Note areas where you did well and areas for improvement.
4. Set a goal to improve one aspect of your communication each week.

Effective communication is a skill that improves with practice. Be patient with yourself and your teen as you work on enhancing your communication.

In the next section, we'll explore how to use these communication skills in collaborative planning and goal-setting with your teen.

Collaborative Planning and Goal Setting

Imagine sitting down with your teen on a Sunday evening, not to lecture or interrogate, but to plan the week ahead together. This collaborative approach can transform how you and your teen tackle challenges and set goals. Let's explore how to make this happen:

Joint Planning Sessions

Regular planning sessions can become a powerful tool for connection and organization. Here's how to make them effective:

1. Set a consistent schedule: Choose a time that works for both of you, perhaps weekly or bi-weekly.
2. Create a comfortable environment: Pick a relaxed setting, like the kitchen table or a cozy corner of the living room.
3. Use the right tools: Have a shared calendar, planner, or digital app ready to use together.
4. Start with a check-in: Begin by asking how your teen is feeling about the upcoming week.
5. Review the previous week: Discuss what went well and what could be improved.
6. Plan for the week ahead: Go through upcoming commitments, deadlines, and goals.

These sessions aren't just about planning - they're about building a partnership with your teen.

Shared Responsibility

Empowering your teen to take ownership of their responsibilities is crucial. Here's how to foster shared responsibility:

1. Divide tasks: Let your teen decide which tasks they'll take on and which you'll handle.
2. Guide, don't dictate: Instead of telling your teen exactly what to do, ask questions that help them figure out solutions.
3. Allow for mistakes: Let your teen experience the natural consequences of their choices (within reason).
4. Celebrate successes: Acknowledge when your teen follows through on their commitments.

Visual Planning Tools

Visual aids can make planning more engaging and effective. Try these tools:

1. Shared digital calendars: Use apps like Google Calendar to keep everyone on the same page.
2. Whiteboard planner: Create a large weekly or monthly planner in a common area.
3. Task board: Use a cork board or app like Trello to track tasks moving from "To Do" to "Done."
4. Goal visualization chart: Create a visual representation of progress towards long-term goals.

Regular Reviews and Feedback

Consistent check-ins help keep plans on track and goals in focus. Here's how to make them effective:

1. Schedule weekly reviews: Set aside time to discuss what worked and what didn't.
2. Focus on improvement: Frame challenges as opportunities to adjust and get better.
3. Provide specific feedback: Instead of general praise or criticism, offer concrete observations.
4. Encourage self-reflection: Ask your teen to assess their own progress and challenges.

Here's a practical exercise to get started with collaborative planning:

Family Planning Workshop:

1. Schedule a time for your first planning session.
2. Gather necessary tools (calendar, planner, whiteboard, etc.).

3. Before the session, ask your teen to think about their goals for the upcoming week/month.
4. During the session:
   - Review any existing commitments
   - Discuss your teen's goals and how to achieve them
   - Plan out the week/month together
   - Assign responsibilities
   - Set a time for your next review
5. After a few weeks, evaluate how the process is working and adjust as needed.

The goal is to create a system that works for both you and your teen. Be open to adjusting your approach based on what you learn along the way.

Building Trust and Accountability

Trust is the foundation of a strong parent-teen relationship. But trust isn't given - it's earned through consistent actions and open communication. Here's how to build and maintain trust with your teen:

Establishing Trust

1. Keep your promises: Follow through on what you say you'll do, no matter how small.
2. Be consistent: Apply rules and consequences fairly and consistently.
3. Respect privacy: Give your teen appropriate space and privacy.
4. Admit mistakes: When you mess up, own it and apologize sincerely.

Encouraging Open Communication

1. Share your experiences: Open up about your own challenges and how you've faced them.
2. Be transparent about expectations: Clearly communicate your rules and the reasoning behind them.
3. Create a judgment-free zone: Respond calmly to what your teen tells you, even if it's not what you want to hear.
4. Show appreciation for honesty: Thank your teen for being truthful, especially about difficult topics.

Setting Clear Expectations

Consider creating a family contract that outlines:

- Daily responsibilities (chores, homework, etc.)
- Behavioral expectations
- Consequences for not meeting expectations
- Rewards for consistently meeting expectations

Involve your teen in creating this contract to ensure buy-in and understanding.

Being Accountability Partners

1. Regular check-ins: Set up times to discuss progress on goals and responsibilities.
2. Celebrate achievements: Acknowledge when your teen meets their commitments.
3. Problem-solve together: When goals aren't met, work together to understand why and how to improve.
4. Lead by example: Share your own goals and progress with your teen.

Here's an exercise to build trust and accountability:

Trust-Building Activity:

1. Each family member writes down:
   - One way they'll work to build trust this week
   - One goal they want to achieve
2. Share these with each other
3. At the end of the week, discuss:
   - How did everyone do with their trust-building action?
   - What progress was made on goals?
   - What support is needed for the coming week?

Building trust and accountability is an ongoing process. Consistency and open communication are key to success.

Conflict Resolution Strategies

Conflict is a natural part of any relationship, especially during the teen years. The key is not to avoid conflict, but to handle it constructively. Let's explore some effective strategies:

Understanding Conflict Dynamics

First, it's important to recognize common triggers and patterns in your conflicts:

1. Independence vs. control: Teens push for autonomy while parents try to maintain boundaries.
2. Expectations: Misaligned expectations often lead to frustration on both sides.
3. Communication breakdown: Misunderstandings can escalate into full-blown arguments.
4. Emotional intensity: The teenage brain is still developing, leading to heightened emotional reactions.

Identifying these patterns can help you anticipate and defuse potential conflicts.

Effective Conflict Resolution Techniques

1. Active listening during conflicts:
   - Focus on understanding, not on formulating your response.
   - Repeat back what you've heard to ensure you've understood correctly.
2. Use "I" statements: Instead of: "You never listen to me!" Try: "I feel frustrated when I don't feel heard."
3. Find common ground:
   - Look for areas of agreement, even if they're small.
   - Build on these points of agreement to work towards a solution.
4. Brainstorm solutions together:
   - Encourage your teen to suggest solutions.
   - Be open to compromises that respect both your concerns and your teen's need for independence.

Cooling-Off Periods

Sometimes, emotions run too high for productive discussion. In these cases:

1. Establish a time-out signal: Agree on a word or gesture that either of you can use to pause the conversation.
2. Set a cool-down time: Decide how long you'll take before revisiting the issue (e.g., 30 minutes, a few hours).
3. Use the break constructively: Encourage deep breathing, journaling, or other calming activities during this time.
4. Commit to returning to the conversation: Make sure both parties agree to continue the discussion once emotions have settled.

When to Seek Help

Sometimes, conflicts may require outside assistance. Consider mediation or professional help if:

- Arguments become physically or emotionally abusive.
- The same conflicts keep recurring without resolution.
- There's a complete breakdown in communication.
- Either party feels consistently unheard or misunderstood.

Seeking help is a sign of strength, not weakness. It shows you're committed to improving your relationship.

Here's a practical exercise to improve conflict resolution:

Conflict Resolution Worksheet:

1. Describe a recent conflict:
   - What was it about?
   - What triggered it?
   - How did each person react?
2. Analyze the conflict:
   - What emotions were involved?
   - Were there any misunderstandings?
   - What was each person's underlying need or concern?
3. Brainstorm alternative responses:
   - How could each person have communicated more effectively?
   - What compromise might have worked?
4. Create an action plan:
   - What will you do differently next time a similar situation arises?
   - How can you prevent this type of conflict in the future?

Use this worksheet after conflicts to learn and improve your resolution skills over time.

Family Workshops: Learning Together

Family workshops can be a powerful way to strengthen bonds and develop important skills together. They create a shared learning experience that can be both fun and productive. Here's how to make the most of family workshops:

Time Management Workshops

1. Start by discussing why time management is important for everyone in the family.
2. Have each family member list their daily tasks and commitments.
3. Work together to prioritize these tasks using techniques like the Eisenhower Matrix.
4. Create a family schedule, allocating time for work, school, chores, and leisure.
5. Introduce time management tools like calendars or apps that everyone can use.

Organization and Planning Sessions

1. Choose an area to organize together (e.g., a shared living space, study area).
2. Sort items into categories: keep, donate, discard.
3. Create organizational systems together (e.g., labeled bins, color-coding).
4. Develop a maintenance plan to keep the space organized.
5. Apply these principles to personal spaces and schedules.

Emotional Regulation Exercises

1. Discuss common emotions and stressors that family members experience.

2. Introduce techniques like deep breathing, mindfulness, or journaling.
3. Create a "calm corner" in your home with resources for managing emotions.
4. Role-play scenarios to practice using these techniques in real-life situations.
5. Establish a family check-in routine to discuss emotions and stress levels.

Interactive Activities

1. Role-playing: Act out common family scenarios and practice positive communication.
2. Problem-solving games: Use puzzles or team challenges to develop strategic thinking.
3. Trust-building exercises: Try activities that require cooperation and support.
4. Family goal-setting: Create a family vision board or set collective goals.

The key to successful family workshops is to make them engaging and relevant to everyone. Be open to suggestions and adjust your approach based on what works best for your family.

Here's an idea to get you started:

Family Skills Night:

- Choose one evening a week for family skill-building.
- Rotate responsibility for planning the activity each week.
- Activities could include:
  - Learning a new skill together (e.g., cooking, basic home repairs)
  - Practicing a time management or organization technique
  - Doing an emotional regulation exercise
  - Playing a cooperative game

- After each session, discuss what you learned and how you can apply it in daily life.

By learning and growing together, you not only develop important skills but also strengthen your family bond. These shared experiences can create lasting memories and a foundation of mutual support and understanding.

Real-Life Case Study: Strengthening the Parent-Teen Bond

Meet the Johnson family: Sarah and Mike, and their 15-year-old son, Alex. Once a close-knit unit, they found themselves drifting apart as Alex entered his teenage years. Communication had broken down, with simple conversations often escalating into arguments. Everyone felt frustrated and misunderstood. Let's see how they turned things around:

Initial Challenges:

1. Communication breakdown: Alex responded to questions with shrugs or one-word answers.
2. Constant conflicts: Disagreements about curfew, homework, and screen time were frequent.
3. Lack of trust: Sarah and Mike felt Alex wasn't being honest about his activities.
4. Resistance to family time: Alex avoided family dinners and outings.

Strategies Implemented:

1. Improved Communication:
   - Sarah and Mike practiced active listening, making a conscious effort not to interrupt Alex.
   - They started using open-ended questions: "What was the

most interesting thing that happened at school today?"
instead of "How was school?"

- o They acknowledged Alex's feelings without judgment: "It sounds like you're feeling overwhelmed with all your assignments."

2. Joint Planning Sessions:
   - o The family instituted a Sunday evening planning session.
   - o They used a shared digital calendar to track everyone's commitments.
   - o Alex was encouraged to take the lead in planning his week, with guidance from his parents.

3. Building Trust and Accountability:
   - o Sarah and Mike were transparent about their expectations and the reasoning behind rules.
   - o They created a family contract together, outlining responsibilities and consequences.
   - o Regular check-ins were established to discuss progress on goals and any challenges.

4. Conflict Resolution:
   - o They implemented a "pause button" technique for heated discussions.
   - o Everyone practiced using "I" statements during conflicts.
   - o They worked on finding compromises that respected both Alex's growing independence and his parents' concerns.

5. Family Workshops:
   - o Monthly family skill nights were introduced, rotating responsibility for planning.
   - o They tackled topics like time management, organization, and stress reduction together.

Challenges Faced:

1. Initial resistance: Alex was skeptical about the new approaches at first.
2. Consistency: It was challenging for everyone to stick to the new habits, especially during busy or stressful times.
3. Old patterns: Sometimes, they fell back into old communication patterns during conflicts.
4. Balancing independence: Finding the right balance between guidance and autonomy was an ongoing process.

Adjustments Made:

1. Flexibility: They adjusted the timing of family meetings to accommodate everyone's schedules.
2. Personalization: They tailored communication styles to what worked best for Alex (e.g., sometimes texting instead of face-to-face conversations).
3. Patience: They acknowledged that change takes time and celebrated small improvements.
4. Feedback loop: Regular family check-ins allowed them to tweak their approach based on what was working.

Positive Outcomes:

1. Improved communication: Alex began to open up more, sharing details about his day and his feelings.
2. Reduced conflicts: Arguments became less frequent and were resolved more constructively.
3. Increased trust: Alex felt more comfortable being honest with his parents, even about mistakes.
4. Better time management: The whole family became more organized and less stressed.
5. Stronger bond: Family time became enjoyable again, with everyone actively participating.

Key Takeaways:

1. Consistency is crucial: Sticking to new habits, even when it's challenging, leads to lasting change.
2. Flexibility matters: Being willing to adjust approaches based on what works keeps everyone engaged.
3. It's a team effort: When everyone participates in creating solutions, buy-in increases.
4. Patience pays off: Change doesn't happen overnight, but persistent effort leads to significant improvements.
5. Communication is key: Open, honest, and empathetic communication forms the foundation of a strong family bond.

The Johnson family's journey demonstrates that with commitment, the right strategies, and a willingness to adapt, it's possible to navigate the challenges of the teenage years and emerge with a stronger, more supportive family dynamic.

Wrapping Up

As we conclude this chapter, remember that strengthening your relationship with your teen is an ongoing process. It requires patience, consistency, and a willingness to adapt. Here are some final thoughts to keep in mind:

1. Keep communication channels open: Even when it's challenging, continue to create opportunities for honest, open dialogue.
2. Lead by example: Model the behavior and communication styles you want to see in your teen.
3. Embrace growth: View challenges as opportunities for both you and your teen to learn and grow.
4. Celebrate progress: Acknowledge and appreciate positive changes, no matter how small.

5. Stay committed: Remember that your efforts to build a strong relationship now will pay dividends for years to come.

By implementing the strategies we've discussed - from effective communication techniques to collaborative planning and conflict resolution - you're laying the groundwork for a strong, lasting bond with your teen. This foundation will not only help you navigate the teenage years more smoothly but will also set the stage for a positive relationship well into adulthood.

In the next chapter, we'll explore specialized strategies for teens with ADD/ADHD, providing additional tools to support teens with unique executive functioning challenges. Whether or not your teen has been diagnosed with ADD/ADHD, these strategies can be valuable for any family looking to enhance focus, organization, and overall executive functioning skills.

Specialized Strategies and Professional Insights

Your teen is staring at their homework, fidgeting with their pencil, and glancing at their phone every few seconds. They've been sitting there for an hour, but barely a word has been written. Sound familiar?

For teens with Attention Deficit Hyperactivity Disorder (ADHD), this scenario is all too common. But don't worry - with the right strategies and support, your teen can overcome these challenges and thrive.

In this chapter, we'll explore specialized techniques for teens with ADHD, insights from school counselors, and ways to leverage technology for better executive functioning. Whether your teen has been diagnosed with ADHD or simply struggles with focus and organization, these strategies can make a world of difference.

Tailored Strategies for Teens with ADD/ADHD

Let's start by understanding what ADHD really means. It's not just about being easily distracted or having too much energy. ADHD is a complex neurodevelopmental disorder that affects how the brain processes information and regulates behavior.

ADHD typically manifests in three main ways:

1. Inattention: Difficulty focusing, easily distracted, forgetful in daily activities.
2. Hyperactivity: Constant motion, fidgeting, talking excessively.
3. Impulsivity: Acting without thinking, interrupting others, making rash decisions.

Some teens may primarily struggle with inattention, while others might be more hyperactive. Many have a combination of these symptoms. It's important to remember that ADHD is not a choice or a result of poor parenting - it's a real neurological difference that requires understanding and support.

Now, let's dive into some strategies tailored for teens with ADHD:

Personalized Learning Plans

One size definitely doesn't fit all when it comes to learning with ADHD. That's where personalized learning plans come in. These plans, often formalized as Individualized Education Programs (IEPs) or 504 Plans, are designed to meet your teen's unique needs.

Here's what they might include:

1. Extended time on tests
2. Breaks during long assignments
3. Preferential seating (e.g., away from distractions)
4. Use of assistive technology
5. Modified homework assignments

The key is to work with your teen's school to create a plan that addresses their specific challenges. For example, if your teen struggles with time management, their plan might include using a digital planner with reminders for assignments and deadlines.

Behavioral Interventions

Behavioral strategies can be incredibly effective for teens with ADHD. Here are some techniques to try:

1. Positive reinforcement: Reward desired behaviors to encourage their repetition. This could be as simple as verbal praise or as structured as a token economy system.
2. Token economy: Create a system where your teen earns tokens for completing tasks or demonstrating good behaviors. These tokens can then be exchanged for rewards.
3. Structured routines: Establish consistent daily routines to provide predictability and reduce anxiety.
4. Break tasks into smaller steps: Help your teen tackle big projects by breaking them down into manageable chunks.

Here's an example of how a token economy might work:

Task	Tokens Earned
Completing homework on time	2 tokens
Organizing backpack	1 token
Following morning routine without reminders	2 tokens

Rewards could include extra screen time, a favorite snack, or saving up for a bigger reward like a new game or outing.

Medication Management

For many teens with ADHD, medication can be a game-changer. There are two main types:

1. Stimulants: These are the most commonly prescribed ADHD medications. They work by increasing dopamine levels in the brain, which can improve focus and reduce hyperactivity.
2. Non-stimulants: These are sometimes used if stimulants aren't effective or cause too many side effects. They work differently but can still help manage ADHD symptoms.

It's crucial to work closely with a healthcare provider to find the right medication and dosage. Every teen is different, and what works for one might not work for another. Regular check-ins with the doctor can help monitor effectiveness and manage any side effects.

Medication is not a magic cure-all. It's most effective when combined with behavioral strategies and environmental support.

Here's a practical exercise to help you and your teen track the effectiveness of ADHD strategies:

ADHD Strategy Tracker:

1. Strategy being used (e.g., token economy, medication, structured routine)
2. Start date
3. Daily rating (1-10) of:
   ○ Focus
   ○ Task completion
   ○ Mood
4. Weekly notes on improvements or challenges
5. Adjustments made
6. Overall effectiveness after one month

Use this tracker to see what's working and what might need adjustment. It can also be helpful information to share with your teen's doctor or school counselor.

By implementing these tailored strategies, you can help your teen manage their ADHD symptoms more effectively. Remember, the goal isn't to "fix" your teen - it's to help them develop the skills and strategies they need to thrive with ADHD.

Behavioral Techniques for Improved Focus

Now that we've covered some general strategies for teens with ADHD, let's dive into specific behavioral techniques that can help improve focus and organization. These methods can be beneficial for all teens, but they're especially powerful for those struggling with attention and executive functioning.

Token Economy Systems

Remember when we mentioned token economies earlier? Let's explore this concept in more depth. A token economy is a type of behavioral modification system that rewards desired behaviors with "tokens" that can be exchanged for privileges or rewards.

Here's how to set up a token economy system:

1. Identify target behaviors: Choose specific behaviors you want to encourage. For example:
   ○ Completing homework without reminders
   ○ Staying focused during study time
   ○ Following morning and bedtime routines
2. Assign token values: Decide how many tokens each behavior is worth. More challenging tasks should earn more tokens.
3. Create a reward menu: Work with your teen to create a list of rewards and their "costs" in tokens. This could include:
   ○ 30 minutes of extra screen time (5 tokens)

- Choosing the family movie for movie night (10 tokens)
- A trip to the ice cream shop (15 tokens)

4. Implement consistently: Be sure to award tokens immediately when the desired behavior occurs.
5. Review and adjust: Regularly review the system with your teen and make adjustments as needed.

The key to a successful token economy is consistency and immediate reinforcement. This system can help your teen see the direct connection between their efforts and positive outcomes.

Self-Monitoring Techniques

Teaching your teen to monitor their own behavior can be a powerful tool for improving focus and organization. Here are some self-monitoring techniques to try:

1. Checklists: Encourage your teen to create daily or weekly checklists of tasks they need to complete. The act of checking off completed items can be very satisfying and motivating.
2. Self-assessment forms: Have your teen rate their focus and productivity at the end of each study session or school day. This can help them become more aware of their habits and patterns.
3. Time tracking: Teach your teen to estimate how long tasks will take and then track the actual time spent. This can help improve time management skills.
4. Personal reminders: Encourage your teen to set reminders on their phone or use a planner to keep track of assignments and deadlines.

Here's a simple self-monitoring checklist your teen can use:

Daily Focus Checklist:

- I prepared my study space before starting work
- I put my phone away during study time
- I took short breaks every 30 minutes
- I completed my most important task first
- I asked for help when I needed it

Encourage your teen to reflect on their checklist at the end of each day. What went well? What could be improved tomorrow?

Cognitive Behavioral Strategies

Cognitive Behavioral Therapy (CBT) techniques can be very helpful for teens with ADHD. While it's best to work with a trained therapist for full CBT, there are some strategies you can implement at home:

1. Thought stopping: Help your teen identify negative thought patterns and replace them with more positive, productive thoughts. For example, instead of "I can't do this, it's too hard," encourage them to think, "This is challenging, but I can break it down into smaller steps."
2. Cognitive restructuring: Teach your teen to challenge irrational thoughts and look for evidence that contradicts negative beliefs.
3. Mindfulness practices: Simple mindfulness exercises can help improve focus and reduce anxiety. Try guided meditations or deep breathing exercises with your teen.

The goal of these strategies is to help your teen develop better self-awareness and control over their thoughts and behaviors. It takes time and practice, so be patient and celebrate small improvements along the way.

Environmental Modifications

Sometimes, small changes to the environment can make a big difference in focus and productivity. Here are some modifications to consider:

1. Create a quiet study area: Designate a specific space for homework and studying, free from distractions like TV or high-traffic areas of the house.
2. Use visual aids: Implement visual schedules, to-do lists, or color-coded systems to help your teen stay organized.
3. Provide fidget tools: For teens who need to move to focus, provide stress balls, fidget spinners, or other quiet manipulatives.
4. Optimize lighting: Ensure the study area has good lighting to reduce eye strain and maintain alertness.
5. Consider noise-canceling headphones: These can be helpful for teens who are easily distracted by background noise.

Here's a quick activity to get your teen involved in optimizing their study space:

Study Space Makeover:

1. Have your teen list what distracts them most when studying.
2. Brainstorm solutions for each distraction.
3. Implement changes to the study space based on these solutions.
4. After a week, evaluate what's working and what needs further adjustment.

By involving your teen in this process, you're teaching them to be proactive about creating an environment that supports their focus and productivity.

What works for one teen might not work for another. The key is to experiment with different techniques and modifications until you find what works best for your teen. In the next section, we'll explore how school counselors can provide additional support and insights for teens with ADHD and executive functioning challenges.

Professional Insights from School Counselors

School counselors can be invaluable allies in supporting teens with ADHD and executive functioning challenges. They offer a unique perspective, seeing your teen in the school environment and understanding the academic and social demands they face. Let's explore how school counselors can help and what insights they can provide.

The Role of School Counselors

School counselors wear many hats when it comes to supporting teens with ADHD:

1. Academic support: They help students develop effective study habits, manage their time, and set achievable goals.
2. Emotional and social guidance: Counselors provide a safe space for teens to express their feelings and work through challenges.
3. Liaison between teachers and parents: They facilitate communication to ensure everyone is on the same page regarding your teen's needs and progress.
4. Advocate for accommodations: Counselors can help implement and adjust IEPs or 504 plans.

Counselor Strategies

School counselors have a toolkit of strategies to support executive functioning. Here are some common approaches:

1. Goal-setting sessions: Counselors help teens break down long-term goals into manageable steps. For example, if your teen wants to improve their grades, a counselor might help them set specific goals for each subject and create action plans to achieve them.
2. Time management workshops: These sessions teach students how to prioritize tasks, use planners effectively, and avoid procrastination.
3. Social skills groups: For teens who struggle with social aspects of ADHD (like impulsivity in conversations), these groups provide a safe space to practice social skills.

Here's an example of how a counselor might break down a goal with your teen:

Goal: Improve Math Grade from C to B

1. Attend all classes and pay attention (2 weeks)
2. Complete all homework assignments on time (1 month)
3. Seek help during teacher's office hours for difficult topics (ongoing)
4. Study for tests at least 3 days in advance (for each test)
5. Review progress with counselor bi-weekly

Collaborative Approach

The most effective support comes when school counselors, teachers, and parents work together. Here's how to foster this collaboration:

1. Regular communication: Set up a system for sharing updates, whether it's weekly emails or monthly check-ins.
2. Joint meetings: Attend meetings with your teen's counselor and teachers to discuss progress and challenges.
3. Shared responsibility: Work with the school team to determine who will handle different aspects of support. For example, the counselor might work on organizational strategies, while you focus on creating a structured home environment.

Accessing School Resources

School counselors can help you navigate the resources available at your teen's school. Here's what to ask about:

1. Assessments and evaluations: Schools can often provide or recommend evaluations to better understand your teen's needs.
2. Support groups: Many schools offer groups for students with ADHD or executive functioning challenges.
3. School-based interventions: Ask about programs like study skills classes or peer tutoring.
4. Community resources: Counselors often have information about local therapists, ADHD coaches, or support groups.

Here's a quick checklist for your next meeting with the school counselor:

School Counselor Meeting Checklist:

- Discuss current academic performance
- Review existing accommodations and their effectiveness
- Explore additional support options
- Set goals for the next term
- Schedule next check-in

School counselors are there to help. Don't hesitate to reach out and utilize their expertise in supporting your teen's executive functioning skills.

Leveraging Technology for Executive Functioning

In our digital age, technology can be both a blessing and a curse for teens with executive functioning challenges. When used mindfully, however, tech tools can significantly support organization, time management, and focus. Let's explore how to leverage technology effectively.

Educational Apps

There's an app for almost everything these days, including executive functioning support. Here are some top picks:

1. Todoist: A powerful task management app that helps break down projects, set deadlines, and track progress.
2. MyHomework Student Planner: Keeps track of classes, assignments, and tests with helpful reminders.
3. Evernote: Great for note-taking and organizing information across devices.

4. Forest: Encourages focus by gamifying the process of staying off your phone.

Encourage your teen to try different apps and find what works best for them. The key is consistency in using the chosen tools.

Assistive Technology

For teens who struggle with specific aspects of executive functioning, assistive technology can be game-changing:

1. Speech-to-text software: Helps teens who have difficulty with writing or typing to get their thoughts down quickly.
2. Text-to-speech tools: Can help with reading comprehension by allowing teens to listen to text.
3. Digital highlighters and annotation tools: Make it easier to organize and remember important information from digital texts.
4. Smart pens: Record audio while taking notes, allowing students to review lessons later.

Online Resources and Communities

The internet offers a wealth of resources for teens with ADHD and their parents:

1. ADDitude Magazine (additudemag.com): Offers articles, webinars, and forums on ADHD and executive functioning.
2. Understood.org: Provides information and strategies for learning and attention issues.
3. CHADD (chadd.org): Children and Adults with Attention-Deficit/Hyperactivity Disorder offers support and resources.

These online communities can provide valuable insights, support, and a sense of connection for both you and your teen.

Balancing Technology Use

While technology can be helpful, it's crucial to use it mindfully. Here are some tips for healthy tech habits:

1. Set screen time limits: Use built-in tools on devices or apps like OurPact to manage screen time.
2. Create tech-free zones: Designate certain areas (like the dinner table) or times as device-free.
3. Model good habits: Demonstrate healthy technology use yourself.
4. Encourage offline activities: Balance tech use with physical activities, face-to-face social time, and offline hobbies.

Here's a simple tech use agreement you can create with your teen:

Technology Use Agreement:

1. Homework time: Phones in a designated basket, only educational apps allowed on computer
2. Dinner time: No devices at the table
3. Bedtime: All devices charged outside the bedroom
4. Weekend reward: Extra 30 minutes of recreational screen time for meeting weekly goals

The goal is to use technology as a tool to enhance executive functioning, not as a crutch or distraction. With the right approach, tech can be a powerful ally in supporting your teen's development.

Creating a Supportive Home Environment

While school strategies and technology are important, the home environment plays a crucial role in supporting your teen's executive functioning skills. Let's explore how to create a home atmosphere that nurtures these skills.

Structuring the Home Environment

1. Establish consistent routines: Create a daily schedule that includes regular times for waking up, meals, homework, and bedtime. Consistency helps reduce anxiety and improves time management.
2. Create dedicated study spaces: Designate a quiet, well-lit area for homework and studying. Ensure it's stocked with necessary supplies and free from distractions.
3. Implement organizational systems: Use labeled bins, color-coded folders, or digital organization tools to keep everything in its place.
4. Visual reminders: Use whiteboards, bulletin boards, or digital displays to keep important information visible.

Here's a sample daily routine to consider:

6:30 AM - Wake up, morning routine 7:30 AM - Breakfast 8:00 AM - School 3:30 PM - After-school snack & short break 4:00 PM - Homework time 6:00 PM - Free time/extracurriculars 7:00 PM - Dinner 8:00 PM - Evening routine, pack bag for tomorrow 9:00 PM - Wind-down time (no screens) 9:30 PM - Bedtime

Family Involvement

1. Regular family meetings: Hold weekly meetings to discuss schedules, challenges, and successes.
2. Collaborative planning: Work with your teen to plan their week, set goals, and prioritize tasks.
3. Shared responsibilities: Assign household tasks to build a sense of responsibility and accomplishment.
4. Lead by example: Model good organizational and time management habits yourself.

Promoting Positive Behavior

1. Use praise effectively: Offer specific, sincere praise for effort and progress, not just outcomes.
2. Set clear expectations: Clearly communicate your expectations for behavior and responsibilities.
3. Consistent consequences: Follow through with agreed-upon consequences when expectations aren't met.
4. Reward system: Consider implementing a reward system for meeting goals or consistently following routines.

Providing Emotional Support

1. Practice active listening: Give your teen your full attention when they're speaking to you.
2. Validate feelings: Acknowledge your teen's emotions without judgment.
3. Encourage open communication: Create an environment where your teen feels safe sharing their thoughts and feelings.
4. Offer help, don't impose: Ask, "How can I support you?" instead of jumping in with solutions.

Remember, creating a supportive home environment is an ongoing process. Be patient with yourself and your teen as you work together to find what works best for your family.

Real-Life Case Study: Specialized Success Stories

Let's meet Jason, a 15-year-old diagnosed with ADHD. Jason struggled with staying focused on schoolwork, often felt overwhelmed by assignments, and had difficulty managing his time. His grades were slipping, and his confidence was waning.

Initial Challenges:

- Difficulty starting and completing homework
- Easily distracted in class
- Trouble organizing school materials
- Low self-esteem due to academic struggles

Strategies Implemented:

1. Personalized Learning Plan:
   - Extended time on tests
   - Use of a quiet study room for exams
   - Permission to use fidget tools in class
2. Behavioral Interventions:
   - Implemented a token economy system at home
   - Broke down assignments into smaller, manageable tasks
   - Used a timer for focused work sessions (Pomodoro Technique)
3. Technology Support:
   - Introduced a digital planner app for organizing assignments
   - Used text-to-speech software for reading assignments
   - Implemented website blockers during study time
4. Home Environment Changes:
   - Created a dedicated, clutter-free study space
   - Established a consistent daily routine
   - Implemented a visual schedule for daily tasks
5. School Collaboration:
   - Regular check-ins with school counselor
   - Teacher updates on assignment progress
   - Participation in a school-based social skills group

Challenges Faced:

- Initial resistance to new routines and tools
- Inconsistent use of strategies when stressed
- Difficulty balancing increased structure with desire for independence

Adjustments Made:

- Simplified digital planner to focus on most critical tasks
- Introduced short, frequent breaks during study sessions
- Gradually increased responsibility for managing own schedule

Positive Outcomes:

- Improved grades across all subjects
- Enhanced ability to start and complete assignments independently
- Increased confidence and positive self-image
- Better time management skills
- Improved relationships with teachers and peers

Key Takeaways from Jason's Story:

1. Personalized approach: What works for one teen may not work for another. Tailoring strategies to Jason's specific needs was crucial.
2. Consistency is key: Regular use of strategies, even when challenging, led to significant improvements over time.
3. Collaboration matters: Working together with school staff ensured consistent support across all environments.
4. Technology can be a powerful tool: When used mindfully, tech tools significantly supported Jason's organization and focus.

5. Patience and flexibility are essential: Progress wasn't linear, and strategies needed adjustment along the way.
6. Building on successes: Small wins boosted Jason's confidence, motivating him to continue using helpful strategies.

Jason's journey demonstrates that with the right support and strategies, teens with ADHD can overcome executive functioning challenges and thrive both academically and personally.

Wrapping Up

As we conclude this chapter, remember that supporting a teen with executive functioning challenges is a journey, not a destination. It requires patience, consistency, and a willingness to adapt. Here are some final thoughts to keep in mind:

1. Celebrate progress: Acknowledge and appreciate improvements, no matter how small.
2. Stay flexible: Be ready to adjust strategies as your teen's needs evolve.
3. Maintain open communication: Keep the dialogue open with your teen, their teachers, and other support professionals.
4. Take care of yourself: Supporting a teen with executive functioning challenges can be demanding. Make sure to practice self-care and seek support when needed.
5. Keep learning: Stay informed about new strategies and resources that could benefit your teen.

By implementing the strategies we've discussed - from personalized learning plans to leveraging technology and creating a supportive home environment - you're providing your teen with the tools they need to succeed. Remember, the goal isn't perfection, but progress and increased independence.

A Chance to Pay It Forward

As you turn the last pages of this book, please take a moment to hold the door open for someone else – for another parent that may be experiencing similar challenges with their teen.

Simply by sharing one to two sentences about your own journey with your teen, you'll show new readers where they can find all the guidance they need to boost their teens' executive functioning skills too.

Please scan the QR code to leave a review.

Thank you so much for your support. We're all on our own parenting journey, but every ounce of help we can share makes a huge impact to our future generation.

Conclusion

As we reach the end of our journey through the world of executive functioning skills, let's take a moment to reflect on why these skills are so crucial for your teen's success, both now and in the future.

Think of executive functioning skills as the control center of your teen's brain. They're the skills that help your teen:

- Plan and organize their day
- Focus on important tasks
- Remember key information
- Juggle multiple responsibilities
- Make good decisions
- Regulate their emotions

By helping your teen develop these skills, you're not just setting them up for academic success - you're equipping them with tools they'll use throughout their lives.

Throughout this book, we've broken down complex concepts into manageable pieces. Let's recap some of the key takeaways:

1. Understanding Executive Functioning: We've explored what these skills are and why they matter.
2. Getting Organized: We've discussed tools like daily planners, checklists, and the power of a clutter-free environment.
3. Time Management: Remember the Pomodoro Technique? We've covered strategies to help your teen make the most of their time.
4. Emotional Regulation: We've explored techniques for managing stress and building resilience.
5. Enhancing Focus: From creating distraction-free zones to understanding the importance of sleep and nutrition, we've covered ways to boost attention.
6. Goal Setting and Prioritization: We've talked about setting SMART goals and balancing short-term and long-term objectives.
7. Parent-Teen Collaboration: We've discussed how to communicate effectively and work together with your teen.
8. Specialized Strategies: For teens with ADHD or other challenges, we've explored tailored approaches and professional insights.

Remember, improving executive functioning skills is a journey, not a destination. It's okay if your teen doesn't master everything at once. The key is consistent effort and patience.

Here's a simple plan to get started:

1. Choose one strategy from the book to implement this week.
2. Discuss it with your teen and agree on how you'll put it into practice.
3. Try it out for a week, then reflect together on what worked and what didn't.
4. Adjust as needed and keep going!
5. After a month, choose another strategy to add to your toolkit.

Remember to celebrate small victories along the way. Did your teen remember to use their planner all week? That's worth a high five! Did they break down a big project into smaller steps? Time for a special treat!

As we wrap up, I want to thank you for your commitment to your teen's growth. Your dedication is the foundation of their success. With the right strategies and consistent support, every teen has the potential to develop strong executive functioning skills.

Remember, you're not just helping your teen succeed in school - you're setting them up for a lifetime of success. Whether they're managing a complex project at work, juggling family responsibilities, or pursuing their dreams, the skills you're helping them develop now will serve them well into the future.

Thank you for allowing me to be a part of this journey with you. Here's to your teen's bright and promising future!

References

ActiveCollab. (n.d.). 8 steps to break down tasks into manageable pieces. https://activecollab.com/blog/project-management/break-down-tasks

Asana. (n.d.). The Eisenhower Matrix: How to prioritize your to-do list. https://asana.com/resources/eisenhower-matrix

Bright Futures NY. (n.d.). How to help teens manage academic pressure. https://www.brightfuturesny.com/post/help-teens-manage-academic-pressure

Business.com. (n.d.). Best tools for setting and tracking goals. https://www.business.com/articles/11-best-tools-for-setting-and-tracking-goals/

Center on the Developing Child at Harvard University. (n.d.). What is executive function? How does it relate to child development? https://developingchild.harvard.edu/resources/what-is-executive-function-and-how-does-it-relate-to-child-development/

Child Mind Institute. (n.d.). Tips for communicating with your teen. https://childmind.org/article/tips-communicating-with-teen/

College of Western Idaho. (n.d.). What is the Pomodoro Technique? A college student's guide. https://cwi.edu/news/blog/what-pomodoro-technique-college-students-guide

Cortés Pascual, A., Moyano Muñoz, N., & Quílez Robres, A. (2019). The Relationship Between Executive Functions and Academic Performance in Primary Education: Review and Meta-Analysis. *Frontiers in Psychology, 10*(10). https://doi.org/10.3389/fpsyg.2019.01582

DuPaul, G. J., Kern, L., Belk, G., Custer, B., Daffner, M., Hatfield, A., & Peek, D. (2018). Face-to-face versus online behavioral parent training for young children at risk for ADHD: Treatment engagement and outcomes. Journal of Clinical Child & Adolescent Psychology, 47(sup1), S369-S383. https://doi.org/10.1080/15374416.2017.1342544

Edutopia. (n.d.). Teaching more efficiently with checklists. https://www.edutopia.org/article/using-checklists-classroom-enhance-efficiency/

Family Education. (n.d.). 22 super helpful apps for kids with ADHD. https://www.familyeducation.com/kids/neurodiversity/adhd/22-super-helpful-apps-for-kids-with-adhd

Gottman Institute. (n.d.). Building trust with teenagers. https://www.gottman.com/blog/building-trust-with-teenagers/

Independent. (n.d.). 7 expert tips to help kids and teens declutter. https://www.independent.co.uk/life-style/teenagers-joy-b2196710.html

Life Skills Advocate. (n.d.). 13 practical time management skills to teach teens. https://lifeskillsadvocate.com/blog/13-practical-time-management-skills-to-teach-teens/

Lilac Center. (n.d.). 8 tips on how to help a teen regulate their emotions. https://www.lilaccenter.org/blog/8-tips-on-how-to-help-a-teen-regulate-their-emotions

Madore, K. P., & Wagner, A. D. (2019). Multicosts of Multitasking. *Cerebrum: The Dana Forum on Brain Science, 2019.* https://www.ncbi.nlm.nih.gov/pmc/articles/PMC7075496/

Mindset Works. (n.d.). How parents can instill a growth mindset at home. https://www.mindsetworks.com/parents/growth-mindset-parenting

Pathway College. (n.d.). How to create a distraction-free study zone. https://www.pathwayscollege.edu/online-college-pasadena/how-to-create-a-distraction-free-study-zone-2/

Psychology Today. (2022, October 3). 8 ways to help your teen stop procrastinating. https://www.psychologytoday.com/us/blog/promoting-empathy-your-teen/202210/8-ways-help-your-teen-stop-procrastinating

Raising Children Network. (n.d.). Conflict management with pre-teens and teenagers. https://raisingchildren.net.au/teens/communicating-relationships/communicating/conflict-management-with-teens

River Software. (n.d.). Balancing act: How to manage short term and long term goals. https://www.riversoftware.com/productivity/balancing-act-how-to-manage-short-term-and-long-term-goals/

Sabrina's Organizing. (n.d.). Teen academic planner to master time management. https://sabrinasorganizing.com/academic-planner-for-teens/

Smart Kids with Learning Disabilities. (n.d.). Teens and executive function skills. https://www.smartkidswithld.org/getting-help/executive-function-disorder/teens-and-executive-function-skills/

Teaching Channel. (n.d.). Bite-sized goal setting with micro-goals. https://www.teachingchannel.com/k12-hub/downloadable/bite-sized-goal-setting-with-micro-goals/

The Blue Heart Foundation. (n.d.). SMART goals and your teen. https://theblueheartfoundation.org/smart-goals-and-your-teen/

U.S. Department of Health & Human Services. (n.d.). Joint planning. https://eclkc.ohs.acf.hhs.gov/family-engagement/home-visitors-online-handbook/joint-planning

Understood. (n.d.). 10 common executive function assessments parents should know about. https://adayinourshoes.com/executive-function-assessment/

Social Skills for Teens

A PARENT'S GUIDE TO HELPING TEENS
OVERCOME CHALLENGES WITH ONLINE
COMMUNICATION, SOCIAL ANXIETY, SELF
ESTEEM, AND PEER PRESSURE

Amber Preston

Introduction

In today's digital age, where emojis often replace genuine emotions and online comments substitute for face-to-face conversations, the art of authentic connection seems to be fading into the background, especially for our teenagers. As someone who has dedicated years to understanding and enhancing adolescents' social skills, I've witnessed firsthand the unique challenges that come with growing up in this digital whirlwind.

My journey into this field wasn't a coincidence, but a path paved as I've watched teenagers show up and wrestle with the messy reality of human connection in both digital and face-to-face spaces. Through their struggles and successes, I realized there was an urgent need for a guide that addresses the nuances of modern communication and the social challenges teens face today.

This book is born from that realization—a toolkit designed to bridge the gap between digital natives and their parents. What sets this resource apart is its focus on practical, actionable advice for identifying the root causes of social anxiety, cultivating empathy, and fostering genuine connections. The innovative "Adult-Teen Exercises" at the end of each chapter provide a unique opportunity for parents and teens to grow together.

So, why did you pick up this book? Ask yourself:

- Do you worry about your teen's ability to form meaningful relationships in a world dominated by screens?
- Are you concerned that your child might be missing out on crucial social skills due to excessive online interaction?
- Do you want to help your teen navigate the complexities of modern social dynamics but feel ill-equipped to do so?

If you answered yes to any of these questions, then this guide has found its way to you for a reason. As a parent, you have unique concerns that keep you up at night. Whether it's quiet dinners, closed bedroom doors, or fears about your child losing real human contact, this book is designed specifically with you and your concerns in mind.

Throughout these pages, we'll explore key social skills vital to any teenager's development. Each skill is supported by engaging activities that guarantee not just learning, but also connection. The compelling statistics and heartwarming anecdotes sprinkled throughout aren't just numbers or stories—they're windows into the realities faced by families worldwide, including yours.

This isn't just a book to read; it's a manual to interact with. The "Adult-Teen Exercise" sections provide opportunities for you and your teen to connect, learn, and grow together. By applying the tools and tips discussed here, you can expect to see real improvements in your teenager's confidence, interactive abilities, and overall happiness.

I'm inviting you to join me in this work. This is your chance to profoundly shape how your child connects and thrives. Together, we can nurture honest, grounded relationships in our screen-filled world.

Are you ready to help your teen tap into their authentic social self? Turn the page, and let's begin. It won't always be smooth sailing, but that's where growth happens.

ONE

The Digital Age and Its Impact

D id you know that the average teen spends up to nine hours daily on screens, with a significant chunk devoted to social media and messaging apps? This isn't just a statistic; it's a window into how profoundly the digital world has reshaped the way our teens communicate and connect. The shift from lively dinner table conversations to silent, screen-focused gatherings isn't just a change in dynamics; it's a complete overhaul of communication practices that previous generations could hardly imagine. Understanding these changes and adapting our approach as parents is crucial in fostering healthy communication habits and maintaining strong connections with our kids.

In this chapter, we'll learn about the various facets of this digital revolution and its impact on our teens' lives. From the emergence of new communication platforms to the challenges of maintaining a healthy online-offline balance, we'll navigate the complexities of raising teens in the digital age. Let's get started and uncover the tools and strategies we need to guide our children through this ever-evolving landscape.

The Shift to Online Communication: Navigating the New Norm

The digital revolution has fundamentally altered the way our teens interact with the world around them. As parents, it's crucial that we understand this shift to effectively guide our children through the complexities of modern communication. Let's examine the key aspects of this new norm and how we can adapt our parenting strategies accordingly.

With the rise of digital platforms, teen communication has undergone a seismic shift. Instagram, Snapchat, TikTok, and WhatsApp aren't just apps—they're the primary tools for adolescent interactions. This shift isn't merely about technology replacing traditional forms of communication; it represents a fundamental change in how teens develop socially. These platforms aren't just stages for socializing; they're arenas where social skills are shaped and tested.

As we move forward, it's important to recognize that these digital platforms are more than just passing trends. They're the new social playground for our teens, and understanding their role is crucial for effective parenting in the digital age.

The transition from direct conversations to digital exchanges has significant implications for developing social skills. In digital communications, the immediate feedback loop that face-to-face interaction provides—through gestures, facial expressions, and tone - is often diluted or entirely absent. This can lead to misunderstandings and a decrease in the ability to read emotional cues, which are essential for developing empathy and maintaining relationships.

Recognizing these changes in communication patterns allows us to better understand the challenges our teens face in developing and maintaining relationships in the digital world. It also highlights the importance of ensuring they have opportunities for face-to-face interactions to develop well-rounded communication skills.

Navigating this new norm goes beyond monitoring screen time or supervising social media accounts; it requires a fundamental understanding of the digital landscape and its language. Start by engaging with the platforms your teen uses—not to spy, but to understand the context and nuances of their digital interactions. This engagement can help bridge the generational gap, offering insights into your teen's social world.

By adapting to this digital landscape ourselves, we're better equipped to guide our teens through it. This approach allows us to have more informed and meaningful conversations about their online experiences.

To foster healthier online habits, encourage your teens to engage in meaningful digital interactions that enrich their lives. Discuss the importance of quality over quantity in online communications, emphasizing connections that foster positive feedback and authentic interactions. You can also co-create a digital wellness plan that includes scheduled offline times, ensuring that digital habits align with overall well-being.

As we move forward, remember that promoting healthy online habits is an ongoing process. It requires open communication, flexibility, and a willingness to learn and adapt alongside our teens.

Understanding Social Media's Role in Your Teen's Life

Social media has become an integral part of our teens' lives, shaping their social interactions, self-expression, and identity formation. To effectively guide our children through this digital landscape, we need to understand the multifaceted role that social media plays in their world. Let's examine the various aspects of social media's influence and how we can help our teens navigate this complex terrain.

For today's teens, social media isn't just a platform; it's a vibrant ecosystem where they thrive, socialize, and express themselves. It serves as a social life line that goes beyond mere entertainment—it's where identities are forged and reshaped. In these digital spaces, teenagers find a venue for connection that transcends the physical boundaries of their local environment.

Understanding social media's role as a social lifeline helps us appreciate its significance in our teens' lives. This perspective allows us to approach discussions about social media use with empathy and insight.

However, the pervasive influence of social media comes with its own set of challenges. The platform that allows teens to connect and explore can also expose them to the pressures of comparison culture, where the curated highlights of others' lives can lead to unrealistic standards for personal achievement and happiness. This phenomenon can skew one's self-perception and exacerbate underlying insecurities.

Recognizing both the benefits and potential pitfalls of social media use is crucial. It allows us to have balanced conversations with our teens about their online experiences and helps us guide them towards healthy digital habits.

Navigating these interactions and influences requires a nuanced approach that goes beyond simply monitoring social media usage. The goal is to mentor rather than monitor, guiding teens through the intricacies of online interactions without making them feel surveilled. It's about fostering an environment where teens feel comfortable sharing their online experiences, allowing you to provide guidance and support when they encounter challenging situations.

By shifting our approach from monitoring to mentoring, we can build trust and open communication with our teens about their online lives. This approach allows us to be more effective in guiding them through the digital landscape.

Encourage teens to gravitate towards positive online communities—spaces that affirm their worth, respect their ideas, and foster constructive interactions. Help them explore various platforms to identify communities that align with their interests and values, whether it's art, music, science, or social activism.

Remember that understanding social media's role in your teen's life is an ongoing process. Stay curious, keep the lines of communication open, and be ready to adapt your approach as the digital landscape continues to evolve.

Digital Etiquette: Teaching Respect and Kindness Online

In the digital world, where face-to-face interactions are often replaced by screen-to-screen communications, teaching our teens about digital etiquette is more important than ever. This section will explore how we can instill values of respect, kindness, and responsible behavior in our teens' online interactions. Let's learn more about the key aspects of digital etiquette and how we can effectively teach these crucial skills.

Digital citizenship is a crucial framework for guiding behavior in this connected world. It encompasses aspects like digital literacy, ethics, etiquette, and online safety. Understanding and embracing good digital citizenship is essential because it sets the tone for how individuals, especially vulnerable teens, interact in their digital worlds.

By emphasizing the importance of digital citizenship, we lay the foundation for responsible and respectful online behavior. This understanding helps our teens navigate the digital world with confidence and integrity.

In an era where empathy can sometimes be diluted by the digital divide—where screens shield us from the immediate emotional reactions of those we interact with—it's crucial to actively cultivate a sense of empathy and respect in online interactions. Remind your teen that there's always a real person behind the screen, with feelings, hopes, and vulnerabilities just like their own. Start by discussing real scenarios teens might encounter online, such as witnessing or experiencing cyberbullying. Ask your child how they would feel if they were to imagine being in the other person's shoes, and discuss the power of words in both positive and negative contexts.

By focusing on empathy, we help our teens develop the emotional intelligence needed to navigate online interactions with kindness and understanding. This skill is invaluable not just in the digital world, but in all aspects of life.

Parents have a unique opportunity to model positive digital conduct. This goes beyond not texting while driving or avoiding oversharing personal information on social media; it's also about demonstrating mindfulness and respect in every digital communication. Show your teen that even a simple 'please' or 'thank you' can change the tone of a digital exchange, and that addressing misunderstandings calmly and clearly can prevent many online conflicts.

Remember, our teens are watching and learning from our online behavior. By setting a positive example, we reinforce the importance of digital etiquette in a powerful and tangible way.

It's inevitable that teens will eventually encounter negative comments or cyberbullying. Teaching them how to handle these experiences constructively is crucial to ensuring they don't become overwhelmed or hurt by such incidents. Encourage your teen to come to you or another trusted adult if they experience anything upsetting online. Discuss strategies for managing negativity, such as not responding to provocative comments, blocking users who are consistently negative, and reporting serious cases of cyberbullying to both platform administrators and, if necessary, local authorities.

Teaching these skills is an ongoing process. Regularly revisit these topics with your teen, and be open to learning from their experiences as well. By fostering a culture of respect and kindness online, we help create a more positive digital world for everyone.

The Balance Between Online and Offline: Finding Harmony

In our increasingly connected world, striking a balance between online engagement and offline activities is crucial for our teens' well-being. It's important to learn about and develop strategies for helping our children find harmony between their digital and real-world experiences. Doing this can encourage a healthy balance that allows our teens to benefit from both worlds.

In the rhythm of our daily lives, where screens often dominate our attention and interactions, the importance of finding balance between digital engagement and the real world couldn't be more significant. While the digital world is rich with information and communities, it can't capture the nuances of human interaction that are only nurtured through face-to-face engagement.

Understanding the need for balance is the first step in helping our teens navigate their online and offline worlds. It sets the stage for creating strategies that promote a well-rounded lifestyle.

Designate specific areas or times of the day as tech-free—for example, during meal times or in the family living room in the evening. This encourages everyone to engage with each other without the distractions of phones, tablets, or laptops. The goal is to create environments that foster connection through conversation, board games, cooking together, or other group activities that encourage cooperation and communication.

By creating these unplugged spaces, we provide opportunities for genuine face-to-face interactions and help our teens develop crucial social skills that can't be replicated online.

Motivating teens to explore real-world hobbies and interests plays a significant role in balancing online and offline activities. Whether it's sports, music, art, or reading, hobbies can significantly enrich a teen's life, providing fulfillment and skills that might not be developed online. Support their endeavors by attending their performances, games, or simply providing the resources they need to pursue these activities.

Engaging in offline hobbies not only provides a break from screen time but also helps teens develop new skills, build confidence, and discover passions that can enrich their lives in meaningful ways.

Encourage your teens to participate in group activities where they can interact with peers in various settings. These could be study groups, community service initiatives, or social gatherings like family get-togethers or neighborhood picnics. Each setting offers different dynamics and opportunities for developing social skills.

Helping your teen find balance requires flexibility, open communication, and a willingness to adjust strategies as they grow and their needs change. By promoting a healthy balance between online and offline activities, we help our teens develop into well-rounded individuals capable of thriving in both digital and real-world environments.

Screen Time vs. Face Time: Encouraging Real Connections

In the age of digital communication, the value of face-to-face interactions can sometimes be overlooked. Helping teens understand the importance of real connections and providing them strategies for encouraging meaningful in-person interactions alongside digital communication is crucial to help our teens strike a balance between screen time and facetime.

In-person interactions foster a range of non-verbal cues that digital communication can't replicate. These include body language, tone of voice, and immediate feedback, all of which are crucial for understanding emotional nuances and developing empathy. When teens interact face-to-face, they learn how to navigate the subtleties of human emotions and reactions, which are essential for building strong personal and professional relationships in the future.

Understanding the unique value of face-to-face communication helps us emphasize its importance to our teens. It sets the stage for encouraging more in-person interactions in their daily lives.

Fostering this balance as parents doesn't mean imposing strict rules that might be met with resistance, but rather guiding your teens with agreed-upon boundaries that they understand and see the value in. One effective strategy is the co-creation of a "family media plan," This plan involves setting clear guidelines for when and where screens can be used at home, as well as ensuring that digital devices don't interfere with sleep, study, or family interaction times.

By involving our teens in the process of setting screen time limits, we empower them to take ownership of their digital habits and understand the importance of balance.

Shifting focus from quantity to quality in digital communication can also significantly enhance relationships. Discuss the importance of being present during digital interactions with your teen. This can mean having more meaningful video calls with family or friends rather than frequent, fragmented text exchanges. Demonstrate the value of full attention during these calls, comparing it to what they would offer someone face-to-face.

Encouraging real connections in a digital world is an ongoing effort, requiring patience, understanding, and a willingness to lead by example. By emphasizing the value of face-to-face interactions and helping our teens find a balance with their screen time, we equip them with the skills they need to build strong, meaningful relationships both online and offline.

Exercise: Digital Wellness Plan

Now that we've explored the various aspects of navigating the digital world, let's put our knowledge into action. This activity is designed to help you and your teen work together to create a personalized approach to digital wellness. It's an opportunity to open up dialogue, set mutual expectations, and create a plan that works for your family.

This activity is not about imposing rules, but rather about collaboratively creating a framework that supports your teen's digital well-being. It's an opportunity to demonstrate that you value their input and trust their judgment, while also providing guidance and support.

Objective

Create a personalized digital wellness plan with your teen to promote healthy online habits and a balanced digital lifestyle.

Instructions

1. Sit down with your teen for an open and honest discussion about their current online activities.

- Ask them what aspects of their digital life they enjoy and find meaningful.
- Encourage them to share any concerns or areas they feel could be improved.

2. Based on your conversation, work together to establish guidelines for healthy digital practices. Consider including:

- Specific times for unplugging, such as during meals, before bedtime, or for a set period each day.
- Ideas for balancing online and offline activities, like setting aside time for hobbies, outdoor play, or face-to-face socializing.
- Strategies for engaging in digital practices that are enriching and meaningful, such as learning a new skill, connecting with friends and family, or exploring creative outlets.

3. Create a shared digital calendar or document where you can record your agreed-upon digital wellness plan.

- Include the specific guidelines, schedules, and activities you've discussed.
- Make sure both you and your teen have access to this plan for easy reference and accountability.

4. Schedule regular check-ins to review the plan together, perhaps once a week or every few weeks.

- Discuss what's working well and what challenges you've encountered.
- Make adjustments to the plan as needed, based on your teen's needs and evolving digital landscape.
- Celebrate successes and encourage open communication about digital wellness.

Reflection

After implementing your digital wellness plan for a month, reflect on the experience together:

- What positive changes have you noticed in your teen's digital habits and overall well-being?
- What strategies have been most effective in promoting a balanced digital lifestyle?
- What areas still need improvement, and how can you continue to support your teen's healthy relationship with technology?

By engaging your teen in open dialogue, setting clear guidelines, and regularly reviewing progress, you can help them develop the skills and mindset needed to navigate the digital world in a healthy, balanced way.

As we conclude this chapter, it's important to remember that navigating the digital world with our teens isn't about being perfect—it's about being present, curious, and open to learning together. The digital landscape is constantly evolving, and so must our approaches to parenting within it. By understanding their digital world, fostering open communication, and working together to create healthy habits, we can help our teens develop the skills they need to thrive both online and offline.

The journey of parenting in the digital age is complex and often challenging, but it's also filled with opportunities for connection, growth, and mutual understanding. As we move forward, let's approach this journey with patience, flexibility, and a commitment to supporting our teens as they navigate the intricate web of digital and real-world interactions. Together, we can help them build the foundation for a balanced, fulfilling life in our increasingly connected world.

TWO

Social Anxiety in Teens

D id you know that about 9% of teens experience social anxiety disorder? (Leigh & Clark, 2018). That's not just a statistic—it's a window into the silent struggle many of our kids face every day. As parents, we often chalk up our teens' reluctance to socialize to typical adolescent awkwardness. But sometimes, it's more than that. It's a deep-seated fear that can profoundly impact their lives.

In this chapter, we'll start to understand social anxiety in teens. We'll learn what it looks like, where it comes from, and most importantly, how we can help our kids navigate through it. Whether your teen is dealing with mild social discomfort or more severe anxiety, you'll find practical strategies and insights to support them on their journey to social confidence.

Identifying Social Anxiety: Signs and Symptoms

Social anxiety isn't just about being shy or introverted. It's an intense, persistent fear of being watched and judged by others. While shyness might make someone uncomfortable in social situations, social anxiety can be debilitating, making even the simplest daily activities feel impossible.

Think about the last time you felt nervous before a big presentation or meeting new people. Now, imagine feeling that level of anxiety every time you step out of the house or interact with others. That's the reality for many teens with social anxiety.

So, what does social anxiety look like in teens? It might show up as:

- Avoiding school or social activities
- Physical symptoms like shaking, sweating, or nausea in social situations
- Difficulty speaking to strangers or authority figures
- Extreme fear of embarrassment or humiliation
- Reluctance to eat in public or use public restrooms
- Refusing to participate in class discussions
- Excessive worry about upcoming social events
- Overanalyzing their performance after social interactions
- Difficulty making eye contact or speaking above a whisper
- Preferring to communicate via text or social media rather than in person

These aren't just occasional nerves—they're persistent fears that don't subside and often worsen over time without intervention.

It's important to note that these symptoms can vary from teen to teen. Some might experience all of these signs, while others might only show a few. The key is to look for patterns and persistence in these behaviors.

The impact of social anxiety on a teen's life can be far-reaching. Academically, they might struggle not because they lack understanding, but because their fear of being called on or presenting in class is paralyzing. They might avoid asking teachers for help, leading to misunderstandings and poor grades. Group projects can become a source of immense stress, potentially affecting not just their own performance but also their relationships with classmates.

Socially, they might have few friends, not because they're uninterested in relationships, but because their fear of social interactions is overwhelming. They might miss out on parties, school dances, or other social events that are crucial for developing social skills and building connections. This isolation can lead to feelings of loneliness and depression, further exacerbating their anxiety.

At home, family dynamics can be affected too. Family gatherings might become a source of tension, with the teen withdrawing or becoming irritable. Parents and siblings might feel frustrated or helpless, not understanding why their loved one is struggling so much with what seems like everyday interactions.

When should you seek help? If you notice your teen consistently avoiding social situations, experiencing intense fear before social events, or if their anxiety is significantly interfering with their daily life, it might be time to consult a professional. Here are some specific signs that professional help might be needed:

- Your teen's anxiety is causing them to miss school regularly
- They're unable to make or maintain friendships due to their anxiety
- Their fears are interfering with family relationships or activities
- They're showing signs of depression or talking about self-harm
- Their anxiety is leading to physical symptoms like chronic headaches or stomach aches
- They're using alcohol or drugs to cope with social situations

Remember, seeking help isn't a sign of weakness or failure. It's a proactive step towards helping your teen live a fuller, happier life. Many teens with social anxiety benefit greatly from cognitive-behavioral therapy, and in some cases, medication might be recommended. A mental health professional can provide a proper diagnosis and create a tailored treatment plan for your teen.

The Roots of Social Anxiety: Understanding Causes

Social anxiety doesn't have a single cause. It's usually a complex interplay of biological and environmental factors. Understanding these root causes can help us approach the problem with more empathy and develop more effective strategies to help our teens.

Some teens might have a genetic predisposition towards anxiety disorders, inheriting a tendency towards heightened emotional sensitivity. This doesn't mean they're destined to develop social anxiety, but it might make them more susceptible to it. It's like having a more sensitive alarm system—their brain might be quicker to perceive social situations as threatening.

Brain chemistry also plays a role. Neurotransmitters like serotonin and dopamine, which regulate mood and emotions, might be imbalanced in individuals with social anxiety. This is why medication that targets these neurotransmitters can sometimes be helpful in treatment.

Environmental influences play a crucial role too. Family dynamics, school experiences, and peer interactions can all contribute to the development of social anxiety. A highly critical home environment, where mistakes are harshly judged, can lead a child to internalize the belief that they're constantly being evaluated negatively by others. Similarly, overprotective parenting might inadvertently send the message that the world is a dangerous place, leading to heightened anxiety in social situations.

Experiences of bullying or social rejection can leave deep emotional scars. A teen who was once mocked for stumbling over their words during a class presentation might develop an intense fear of public speaking. These negative experiences can create a pattern of avoidance, where the teen starts to shy away from similar situations to prevent future embarrassment.

In our digital age, social media's impact on social anxiety can't be overstated. The constant comparison to curated online personas can fuel feelings of inadequacy and anxiety. Teens might feel pressure to present a perfect image online, leading to a disconnect between their online persona and their real-life self. The fear of missing out (FOMO) can drive excessive social media use, paradoxically leading to more anxiety about real-life social interactions.

The instant and often anonymous nature of online communication can make face-to-face interactions feel more daunting. A teen who's used to carefully crafting text messages might feel overwhelmed by the spontaneity required in real-time conversations.

Breaking the cycle of social anxiety involves challenging and reshaping the negative thought patterns that fuel it. Cognitive-behavioral strategies can be particularly effective. These involve identifying negative thoughts that often trigger anxiety, such as "I'll embarrass myself" or "Everyone is judging me," and systematically challenging their validity.

For instance, if your teen thinks, "I always say the wrong thing," you can help them challenge this thought by asking:

- Is this always true? Can you think of times when you've said the right thing?
- What evidence do you have for this thought? Against it?
- If your best friend said they always say the wrong thing, what would you tell them?

By consistently questioning these negative thoughts, teens can start to develop more balanced, realistic perspectives. Over time, this can lead to a reduction in anxiety and an increase in confidence.

Another strategy is gradual exposure. This involves slowly and systematically facing feared social situations, starting with less anxiety-provoking scenarios and working up to more challenging ones. For example, a teen might start by saying hello to one classmate, then progress to having a short conversation, and eventually work up to joining a group activity.

It's important to pair this exposure with relaxation techniques and positive self-talk. Teaching your teen deep breathing exercises or mindfulness practices can give them tools to manage anxiety in the moment. Encouraging them to use affirmations like "I can handle this" or "I am worthy of friendship" can help counteract negative self-talk.

Remember, overcoming social anxiety is a process. It takes time, patience, and consistent effort. But with the right support and strategies, teens can learn to manage their anxiety and develop fulfilling social lives.

Encouraging Social Interaction: Gentle Steps Forward

When it comes to helping teens overcome social anxiety, small steps matter. The idea of attending a party or giving a class presentation might feel overwhelming, but setting micro-goals can lead to significant breakthroughs. It's about building confidence gradually, one small victory at a time.

Start with something as simple as smiling at a classmate or making eye contact. These might seem like tiny actions, but for a teen with social anxiety, they can be significant challenges. Celebrate these small wins—they're the building blocks of social confidence.

Gradually, these small victories can build up to saying hello to a friend, asking a question in class, or joining a group discussion for a few minutes. The key is to set goals that are challenging but achievable. Each success, no matter how small, reinforces the idea that social interactions can be manageable and even enjoyable.

Creating safe social opportunities is crucial. Arrange small gatherings at home where your teen feels comfortable. This could be inviting one or two friends over for a movie night or a gaming session. The familiar environment can help reduce anxiety, allowing your teen to focus on the social interaction itself.

Plan activities that require cooperation but provide enough structure to reduce anxiety. Board games, for instance, offer a structured way to interact while taking the pressure off constant conversation. A pizza-making party combines a fun activity with social interaction, giving your teen something to focus on besides their anxiety.

Extracurricular activities can be a game-changer in developing social skills. Encourage participation in sports, clubs, or arts classes—structured yet informal settings where social interaction is part of the fun. These activities provide natural conversation starters and shared experiences, making it easier to connect with peers.

The key is to encourage activities that genuinely interest your teen, rather than pushing them into popular ones that might feel overwhelming. If your teen loves art, an art club might be less anxiety-provoking than a large team sport. If they're into technology, a robotics club could be a great fit. The shared interest provides common ground, making social interactions feel more natural and less forced.

Practicing social scenarios can also build confidence. Role-play common situations at home, like ordering food at a restaurant, asking a peer about a school assignment, or introducing oneself to a new classmate. This kind of practice can demystify social exchanges and equip your teen with a toolkit of responses they feel prepared to use in real life.

Start with simple scenarios and gradually increase the complexity as your teen's confidence grows. For example, you might start with practicing how to greet someone, then move on to maintaining a short conversation, and eventually work up to more challenging situations like giving a presentation or attending a social event.

Remember, the goal isn't perfection—it's progress. Encourage your teen to focus on their efforts rather than the outcome. Even if an interaction doesn't go as smoothly as they'd hoped, the fact that they tried is a success in itself.

Throughout this process, your support and understanding are crucial. Be patient and empathetic. Acknowledge that what you're asking them to do is challenging. Offer praise for their efforts, not just their successes. Your belief in their ability to overcome their anxiety can be a powerful motivator.

Exercise: Role-Playing for Confidence

Objective

To help teens build confidence and reduce social anxiety through structured role-playing activities.

Background

Role-playing is an effective tool for managing social anxiety. It provides a safe environment for teens to practice social interactions without the pressure of real-world consequences.

Instructions

1. Identify Anxiety-Inducing, Realistic Scenarios

   - Discuss with your teen specific social situations that cause anxiety

2. Examples: speaking in class, making small talk, ordering food

3. Assign Roles

- You play the role of other people in the scenario
- Your teen practices initiating and maintaining conversations

4. Prepare and Practice

- Use props to enhance realism (e.g., textbooks, backpacks)
- Help your teen develop a script or key points to cover
- Encourage improvisation to handle unexpected turns in conversation
- Example Script

  i. Teen: "Hey, I missed yesterday's math class. Could you tell me what the homework assignment was?" Parent (as classmate): "Sure, we had to do problems 1-15 on page 87." Teen: "Thanks! Do you know when it's due?" Parent: "I think it's due on Friday, but you might want to check with Mr. Johnson to be sure." Teen: "Okay, I'll do that. Thanks for your help!"

5. Provide Constructive Feedback

- Highlight positive aspects (e.g., eye contact, clear voice, good questions)
- Gently suggest improvements (e.g., body language, managing filler words)

6. Encourage Self-Reflection

- Ask your teen to assess their performance
- Discuss how they felt during the role-play

7. Gradually Increase Difficulty

- Introduce more challenging scenarios as confidence grows
- Examples: disagreeing respectfully, joining ongoing conversations

8. Maintain a Supportive Atmosphere

- Keep the mood light and encouraging
- Take breaks if your teen becomes overwhelmed

9. Emphasize Transferable Skills

- Discuss how these skills apply to various life situations
- Examples: job interviews, romantic relationships

As your teen becomes more comfortable with basic scenarios, gradually introduce more challenging situations. This could include role-playing how to respectfully disagree with someone, how to join an ongoing conversation, or how to handle a misunderstanding.

The skills developed through role-playing can extend beyond just managing social anxiety. They're valuable life skills that can help your teen in various aspects of their life.

Exercise: Building a Social Skills Action Plan

Objective

To create a personalized, structured plan for teens to develop social confidence and manage anxiety, with parental support.

Materials

- Notebook or digital device for journaling
- Calendar for tracking progress
- Pens/pencils

Instructions

1. Initiate Open Conversation

    - `Create a safe, non-judgmental space
    - Listen actively and empathetically to your teen's concerns about social anxiety

2. Identify Specific Challenges

    - List social situations that cause anxiety (e.g., initiating conversations, participating in family gatherings)
    - Be as detailed as possible to create a targeted plan

3. Set "SMART Goals" by developing goals that are:

    - Specific (e.g., "Say hello to one classmate each day" instead of "Be more social")
    - Measurable (e.g., "Participate in class discussions three times a week")
    - Achievable (e.g., "Have lunch with one friend" rather than "Attend a large party")
    - Relevant (address specific anxiety triggers and align with broader social development)
    - Time-bound (e.g., "By the end of the month, I will have initiated three conversations with peers")

4. Establish a Tracking System

- Set up a journal or log (physical or digital)
- Record:

  - Feelings before and after social interactions
  - What went well
  - What was challenging
  - Insights gained

5. Conduct Regular Reviews

- Schedule weekly check-ins
- Discuss journal entries supportively
- Identify patterns and areas for improvement
- Adjust goals as needed

6. Celebrate Progress

- Acknowledge all successes, no matter how small
- Reinforce positive behavior and boost confidence

7. Implement Reward System

- Define milestones
- Choose appropriate rewards (e.g., favorite treats, activities)

8. Address Setbacks

- Frame difficulties as learning opportunities
- Discuss how to handle similar situations in the future

9. Regularly Revise the Plan

- Be flexible and adapt based on experiences and feedback
- Increase challenge level as confidence grows

10. Provide Ongoing Support

- Offer unconditional encouragement and understanding
- Be available to listen without judgment

Sample Action Plan

Goal 1: Improve comfort in class discussions

- Week 1-2: Raise hand to answer one question per week
- Week 3-4: Contribute one comment to class discussion per week
- Week 5-6: Ask one question during class per week

Goal 2: Expand social circle

- Month 1: Say hello to one new classmate each week
- Month 2: Have a brief conversation with a classmate once a week
- Month 3: Invite a classmate to study together or have lunch

Goal 3: Increase comfort in group settings

- Step 1: Attend a small group activity (e.g., study group) for 30 minutes
- Step 2: Participate in a structured group activity (e.g., board game night)
- Step 3: Attend a larger social event (e.g., school club meeting) for an hour

It's important to acknowledge that progress may not always be linear. There might be days when your teen takes two steps forward and one step back. That's okay. What matters is the overall trajectory and the resilience they're building along the way.

Also, don't forget to take care of yourself during this process. Supporting a teen with social anxiety can be emotionally taxing. Make sure you have your own support system and self-care practices in place.

As we wrap up this chapter, remember that navigating social anxiety with your teen isn't about being perfect—it's about being present, understanding, and supportive. It's about creating a safe space for your teen to challenge themselves, make mistakes, and grow.

By implementing these strategies and maintaining open communication, you can help your teen build the confidence and skills they need to thrive socially. It can feel like a lot, but with patience, consistent effort, and lots of love, your teen can overcome social anxiety and develop fulfilling relationships.

Every small step your teen takes is a victory. Every conversation initiated, every class participated in, every social event attended is a testament to their courage and resilience. As they continue to push their boundaries and expand their comfort zone, they're not just overcoming social anxiety—they're building a foundation for a rich, connected life.

In the next chapter, we'll explore more specific strategies for helping teens build confidence in various social situations. We'll look at how to navigate school life, maintain friendships, and handle social media in a healthy way. But for now, take a moment to appreciate how far you've come in understanding and addressing your teen's social anxiety. You're taking important steps to support your child, and that alone is something to be proud of.

THREE

Communication Skills

I n the unfolding story of adolescence, where every interaction can profoundly impact self-awareness and confidence, the mastery of communication skills remains a crucial chapter. Learning how to appropriately express yourself isn't just about crafting well-rounded sentences or mastering the grammar of emotions; it's about building bridges through the art of listening and understanding—the very foundation of all human relationships. As you guide your teen through the complex social landscapes of their world, teaching them the nuances of effective communication becomes essential. It's about equipping them with the tools not just to speak, but more importantly, to listen, empathize, understand, and transform their interactions into meaningful exchanges.

Listening with Empathy: The First Step to Understanding

Listening is a crucial skill for building strong relationships and understanding others. For teenagers, learning to listen with empathy can make a big difference in how they connect with people and handle social situations. By mastering active listening, your teen can improve their friendships, family relationships, and even how they handle disagreements. Good listening isn't just about hearing words—it's about understanding feelings and showing others that they matter.

While both empathy and sympathy involve responses to the feelings and experiences of others, they differ significantly in their depth and effectiveness. Empathy involves putting yourself in another person's shoes, understanding their feelings and perspectives as if they were your own. In contrast, sympathy is more about feeling sorry for someone's difficulties, which can sometimes create a sense of distance. You can help your teen develop empathy by discussing various scenarios and asking how they would feel in that situation, encouraging them to go beyond surface emotions to a more nuanced understanding of others' experiences.

Active listening is the cornerstone of effective communication, allowing you to fully engage with others' words and meaning. It involves fully concentrating, understanding, responding, and then remembering what is being said. Here are some techniques that can improve your teen's active listening skills:

- Maintaining eye contact: Encourage them to maintain eye contact, which shows interest and respect for the speaker and helps to focus on what's being said.
- Paraphrasing and summarizing: Teach them the subtle art of paraphrasing and summarizing what they've heard. This not only demonstrates that they are paying attention but also helps them grasp the message on a deeper level.
- Asking thoughtful questions: You might also introduce the practice of asking thoughtful questions, which shows engagement and encourages further discussion, making the speaker feel valued and heard.

Modeling active listening in your daily interactions can serve as a powerful teaching tool for your teen. Demonstrate empathy by listening attentively to their concerns without interrupting, showing understanding, and responding appropriately. Discuss the importance of listening not just to respond, but to understand. Turn everyday interactions into opportunities for connection and learning. Additionally, setting up family discussions where everyone gets a chance to speak and be heard can reinforce these skills. During these sessions, emphasize the importance of patience and respect for the speaker, qualities that are essential for active listening.

Empathetic listening can often serve as a bridge over troubled waters of conflict. By genuinely trying to see each party's perspective and emotions, it becomes easier to find solutions that are acceptable to all involved. Teach your teen that in the midst of disagreement, it's crucial to step back and listen with the intent to understand, not to counter-argue. This approach doesn't just de-escalate conflicts; it also strengthens relationships by fostering mutual respect and under-standing. Discuss situations at home where empathetic listening led to peaceful resolutions, and encourage your teen to apply these lessons in their own interactions.

Expressing Themselves: Encouraging Open Dialogue

Fostering an environment where your teen feels confident and comfortable expressing themselves is crucial for their emotional and social development. One of the primary components of such an environment is helping teens build a robust vocabulary for their emotions. Often, teens might feel a surge of emotions but lack the precise words to express them, leading to frustration or misunderstanding. Start by introducing more nuanced emotional words during your conversations. For instance, instead of using broad terms like 'happy' or 'sad', encourage descriptions like 'elated', 'content', 'melancholy', or 'dejected'. You can facilitate this development by creating an 'emotion chart' with words and expressions describing various emotions and placing it somewhere visible in your home. When discussing how events made you or them feel, regularly refer to this chart, which not only expands their emotional vocabulary but also normalizes the discussion of feelings in everyday conversations. This practice helps teens articulate their emotions more accurately, making it easier for them to communicate their inner experiences and needs.

Creating a safe space for sharing is equally essential to encouraging open dialogue. This space is both physical and emotional; it requires an atmosphere where teens know that their feelings and thoughts are respected and valued. Establish specific times and settings that are dedicated to sharing and listening – perhaps a weekly 'family meeting' or a daily chat over dinner where each family member can discuss their day and anything on their mind. During these times, it's crucial to ensure that the environment is free from distractions like cell phones or televisions.

When your teen shares their thoughts, show genuine interest and refrain from judgment or immediate correction. Instead, respond with empathy and validation, demonstrating that you appreciate their willingness to share and that their feelings are important. This consistent practice not only makes your teen feel valued but also teaches them that it's safe to offer their opinions and feelings, a lesson they will carry into other relationships.

Teaching the use of 'I' statements is another powerful tool for helping teens express themselves constructively. These statements focus on the speaker's feelings rather than blaming or criticizing others, which can help prevent conversations from escalating into conflicts. For example, instead of saying, "You never listen to me," a more constructive statement would be, "I feel ignored when I talk and others don't seem to listen." This shift reduces defensiveness in others and empowers the speaker to focus on what they can control – how they express their feelings. Role-play various scenarios with your teen where 'I' statements would be useful. Start with simple, low-stakes situations like expressing disappointment over a canceled plan, and gradually progress to more challenging emotional expressions like feeling hurt by a friend's actions. This gradual escalation allows your teen to become comfortable using 'I' statements in various contexts, enhancing their ability to communicate both assertively and empathetically.

Role-playing, a versatile tool that your teen is already familiar with from previous exercises, can be extended to practice expressing emotions and thoughts constructively. Set up scenarios that your teen is likely to encounter, such as dealing with a misunderstanding with a friend or asking a teacher for help. In these role-plays, encourage your teen to use the emotional vocabulary they've developed and to utilize 'I' statements to express their feelings. Provide feedback, focusing on their choice of words, tone, and body language, ensuring that all elements contribute to a thoughtful and clear expression of their views and emotions.

Exercise: Constructive Expression Role-Play

Objective

To practice expressing emotions and thoughts constructively using role-play scenarios.

Materials

- List of potential scenarios (provided below)
- Emotion vocabulary chart
- Notepad for feedback

Instructions

1. Choose a scenario from the list or create one that's relevant to your teen's experiences.

2. Assign roles: one person plays the teen, the other plays the second character in the scenario.

3. Before starting, remind your teen to:

- Use the emotional vocabulary they've learned
- Utilize 'I' statements to express feelings
- Pay attention to tone of voice and body language

4. Act out the scenario for 3-5 minutes.

5. After the role-play, provide feedback:

- Highlight effective use of emotional vocabulary
- Point out successful 'I' statements
- Discuss tone of voice and body language
- Suggest areas for improvement

6. Switch roles and try another scenario.

Potential Scenarios

1. Explaining to a friend why you're upset about a misunderstanding
2. Asking a teacher for help with a difficult assignment
3. Discussing a curfew extension with a parent
4. Addressing a teammate who isn't pulling their weight on a group project
5. Talking to a sibling about respecting personal space

Tips for Effective Feedback

- Be specific about what worked well
- Offer constructive suggestions for improvement
- Encourage self-reflection: "How do you think that went?"

Practice Schedule

- Aim to do 2-3 role-plays per week
- Gradually increase the complexity of scenarios
- Encourage your teen to apply these skills in daily life

Reflection

After several practice sessions, discuss with your teen:

- How has their comfort level with expressing emotions changed?
- What differences have they noticed in their real-life interactions?
- Which aspects of constructive expression still feel challenging?

This exercise provides your teen with a safe space to experiment with and refine their communication style, which can boost their confidence in handling similar situations in real life. As these practices become more integrated into their daily habits, your teen will find it increasingly natural to open up and express themselves in ways that foster understanding and respect, thus significantly enhancing their relationships.

Non-Verbal Communication: Reading and Responding to Cues

Navigating the nuanced world of non-verbal communication is akin to understanding a silent language that speaks volumes. Body language, facial expressions, and tone of voice are crucial components of this language, each adding layers of meaning to the words spoken. When a teen learns to interpret these cues accurately, it enhances their ability to connect with others, understand unspoken emotions, and respond more empathetically. For instance, a slumped posture might indicate sadness or defeat, while crossed arms could suggest defensiveness or discomfort. Facial expressions can convey a myriad of emotions from joy to sorrow, and even subtle changes can significantly alter the message's impact. Tone of voice, too, plays a vital role—it can communicate sarcasm, anger, affection, or sincerity, often overriding the literal meaning of the spoken words.

Teaching your teen to pay attention to these silent signals requires more than just pointing them out; it involves nurturing observation skills and empathy. Observational skills can be enhanced through games like watching a muted video clip and trying to deduce the context and emotions based solely on body language and facial expressions. Discuss these observations with your teen, sharing insights on what you each perceive and why. This exercise not only sharpens their ability to pick up on non-verbal cues but also encourages them to pay attention to details that might otherwise be overlooked.

The congruence between what is said and how it's said—verbal and non-verbal alignment—is equally crucial. Inconsistencies between the two can lead to confusion and mistrust. For example, if someone says they're fine, but their voice is flat and their shoulders are slumped, non-verbal signals might suggest otherwise. Helping your teen understand this congruence involves analyzing real-life interactions or role-playing exercises where they practice aligning their verbal messages with their non-verbal signals. This could include practicing maintaining an open posture while communicating or ensuring that their facial expression matches the emotion they're expressing. These practices help teens become more authentic communicators and more perceptive listeners, attuned to the true content of what's being communicated.

In the realm of digital interactions, the transmission and interpretation of non-verbal cues undergo a transformation. While digital platforms strip away much of body language and tone, they often leave room for different types of non-verbal communication, such as the timing of responses, the use of emojis, or the choice of words and punctuation—consider a text message that ends in a period versus an exclamation point.

These nuances can drastically alter the perceived tone and intent behind digital communications. Misinterpretations are common without facial expressions and vocal tone, leading to misunderstandings that can escalate into unnecessary conflicts.

To navigate this, discuss with your teen the importance of clarity in their digital communications. Encourage them to consider how their messages might be perceived and to consider adding clarifying comments or questions if a message could be interpreted ambiguously. Also, stress the importance of discussing sensitive topics in person whenever possible, as this allows for a more complete exchange of verbal and non-verbal signals, reducing the likelihood of misunderstandings.

By fostering an awareness and understanding of non-verbal communication, you empower your teen not only to express themselves more effectively but also to enhance their interpretations of others' communications, both in-person and online. This skill set is crucial as it ensures their growth into empathetic, perceptive individuals capable of navigating complex social landscapes with confidence and understanding.

The Art of Small Talk: Practice Makes Perfect

Small talk is often dismissed as mere filler conversation, but it actually plays a significant role in human interaction. For teenagers, mastering small talk is crucial for building deeper relationships and creating new opportunities. It's like getting warmed up before soccer practice, setting the stage for a more detailed conversation. Small talk helps teens connect with others and gradually move on to more substantial topics. By engaging in these seemingly trivial exchanges, teens learn to navigate conversations, understand their peers' interests, and find common ground for deeper connections.

To engage in small talk effectively, start with topics that are relatable and non-controversial. Discuss hobbies, books, movies, or observations about shared experiences. Encourage your teen to ask simple questions like, "Have you read any good books lately?" or "What did you think of the game last night?" Guide them towards open-ended questions that require more than a yes or no answer, which can help the conversation flow more naturally and reveal more about the interests and personalities of those they're engaging with. To make small talk more engaging, stress the importance of showing genuine interest in the other person's opinions and experiences.

Exercise: Small Talk Role-Play

Objective

To practice small talk skills in a safe environment before applying them in real-world situations.

Materials

- List of scenario prompts (provided below)
- Timer
- Notepad for feedback

Instructions

1. Choose a scenario from the list or create one relevant to your teen's life.
2. Set the scene briefly, describing the context and any relevant details.
3. Assign roles: Parent plays a new acquaintance, teen plays themselves.
4. Set a timer for 3-5 minutes and begin the role-play.
5. After the timer ends, spend 5 minutes on feedback and discussion.

6. Switch roles or try a new scenario, aiming for 3-4 practice sessions.

Scenario Prompts

1. Meeting a new student at a school club meeting
2. Talking to a neighbor at a community barbecue
3. Striking up a conversation with a classmate before a sports match
4. Chatting with a friend's cousin at a birthday party
5. Making small talk with a store clerk while shopping

During the role-play, encourage your teen to:

- Use open-ended questions
- Show genuine interest in responses
- Maintain appropriate eye contact
- Use friendly body language

Feedback Guidelines

- Start with positive observations
- Offer specific, constructive suggestions
- Ask your teen for their own thoughts on the interaction

Sample Feedback: "I liked how you asked about their hobbies. Next time, try following up on their answer with another question to show more interest."

Discussion Points

- What felt natural or challenging about the conversation?
- How might this scenario play out differently in real life?
- What strategies could help in moments of awkward silence?

Tips

- Gradually increase the difficulty of scenarios
- Encourage your teen to initiate these practices when they feel ready
- Remind them that it's okay to make mistakes – that's part of learning

Feedback is crucial here; provide gentle guidance on how they can improve their conversational skills, such as using more open-ended questions, showing more interest in the responses they receive, or even how to better use their body language to convey engagement and openness.

Addressing the potential awkwardness of conversations—entering, maintaining, or leaving them—can be a significant concern for teens, who may feel anxious about the possibility of social missteps. Teach your teen that entering a conversation can be as simple as a smile and a greeting, followed by a relevant observation or question that relates to the context or situation. Maintaining the conversation can involve active listening, nodding, or asking follow-up questions based on what the other person says. Exiting a conversation gracefully can be done with polite phrases that signal a conclusion without abruptness, such as "It was great talking with you" or "I hope to hear more about it later." Handling silent moments doesn't have to be daunting; they can be viewed as natural parts of a conversation where both parties are processing the discussion or considering what to say next. Encourage your teen to use pauses as an opportunity to introduce a new topic or ask another question, seamlessly continuing the flow of conversation.

By incorporating these techniques into their social toolkit, your teen can transform small talk from a mere exchange of pleasantries into a powerful component of their communication skills repertoire. Such skills not only enhance their daily interactions but also boost their confidence in managing and nurturing the relationships they will encounter throughout their lives.

Conflict Resolution: Navigating Disagreements Constructively

Conflict is an inevitable part of human interaction, and for teenagers navigating complex social networks, learning to handle disagreements constructively is a crucial life skill. The first step in effective conflict resolution is identifying the root of conflicts. Often, what appears to be the cause of a disagreement is merely a symptom of a deeper issue. Teach your teen to look beyond surface-level arguments and consider underlying emotions, needs, or misunderstandings that might be fueling the conflict. Encourage them to ask themselves and others involved questions like, "What's really bothering me/you about this situation?" or "What need isn't being met here?" This deeper understanding can pave the way for more meaningful resolutions.

When it comes to communicating during conflicts, maintaining calm and being clear are key. Teach your teen strategies for staying composed in heated moments, such as taking deep breaths, calling for a short break if emotions are running high, or using "I" statements to express feelings without accusation. Emphasize the importance of listening actively to the other person's perspective, even if they disagree. Encourage them to paraphrase what they've heard to ensure understanding and show that they're genuinely trying to see the other person's point of view.

Finding common ground is often the bridge to resolution in conflicts. Guide your teen to look for shared values, goals, or interests that can serve as a foundation for working together towards a solution. This might involve asking questions like, "What do we both want to achieve here?" or "Can we agree on the importance of [shared value]?" By focusing on areas of agreement, even small ones, teens can build momentum towards resolving larger disagreements.

Role-playing is an excellent tool for practicing conflict resolution skills in a safe environment. Set up scenarios that mimic real-life conflicts your teen might encounter, such as disagreements with friends, siblings, or even teachers. Take turns playing different roles, allowing your teen to practice both expressing their own needs and listening to others. After each role-play, discuss what went well and what could be improved. Here's an example scenario to get started:

Scenario: Your teen and their friend have a group project due, but they disagree on how to approach it.

Teen: "I think we should focus on creating a visual presentation. It'll be more engaging." Parent (as friend): "But I think a written report would be more thorough and get us a better grade." Teen: "I understand you're concerned about our grade. That's important to me too. Maybe we could find a way to combine both approaches?" Parent: "That's a good point. What if we do a written report but include some visual elements to make it more engaging?" Teen: "I like that idea. We could play to both our strengths that way."

This example demonstrates looking for common ground (concern about grades), expressing understanding of the other's perspective, and working together to find a solution that addresses both parties' concerns.

Let's try it out.

Exercise: Conflict Resolution Role-Play

Objective

To practice handling disagreements constructively through improvised scenarios.

Materials

- Timer
- Notebook and pen for observer

Instructions

1. Divide into groups of three: two participants and one observer.

2. The participants will create their own conflict scenario based on common teen experiences. Spend 2-3 minutes brainstorming a realistic situation.

3. Assign roles based on the scenario they've created. The observer will take notes and time the interaction.

4. Role-play the scenario for 5-7 minutes, focusing on:

- Identifying the root of the conflict
- Using "I" statements
- Active listening
- Finding common ground
- Proposing solutions

5. After the role-play, spend 5 minutes discussing:

- What went well?
- What could have been handled differently?
- How did it feel to be in each role?

6. Switch roles and create a new scenario to repeat the process.

Guidelines for Creating Scenarios

Encourage participants to think of common conflicts teens might face, such as:

- Disagreements with parents about rules or privileges
- Conflicts with friends over misunderstandings or differing opinions

- Issues with teachers or coaches about grades, playing time, or expectations
- Sibling rivalries or disputes

Guidelines for Participants

- Stay in character
- Be open to compromise
- Listen to understand, not just to respond
- Focus on the issue, not personal attacks

Guidelines for Observer

- Note specific phrases or actions that escalate or de-escalate the conflict
- Watch for non-verbal cues
- Time the interaction
- Prepare constructive feedback

Reflection

After completing 2-3 rounds, gather as a larger group to discuss:

- Common challenges in resolving conflicts
- Effective strategies observed
- How these skills can be applied in real-life situations

This exercise allows teens to practice conflict resolution in a safe environment, helping them develop crucial communication and problem-solving skills they can use in various real-life situations. By creating their own scenarios, they can address conflicts that feel most relevant and realistic to their lives.

Bonus: Reflective Journaling Prompt

Consider incorporating a reflective journaling exercise where, after each role-play session, your teen writes about the experience. They should note what techniques worked, how they felt during the conflict, and what they might do differently next time. This reflection can deepen their understanding of conflict dynamics and their personal conflict resolution style, fostering ongoing learning and improvement in their communication skills.

To bridge the gap between practice and real-life application, encourage your teen to identify one upcoming social situation where they can apply these skills in the short term, such as a group project at school or a family gathering. For a long-term approach, suggest they keep a "real-life authenticity journal" where they document instances of staying true to themselves in social situations, reflecting on their successes and areas for improvement. This ongoing practice will help solidify their ability to navigate social pressures authentically in various real-world contexts.

As we close this chapter and look ahead, the skills your teen has begun to develop will be put into action as we explore more about building confidence and leadership in the following chapters. These next steps are not just about avoiding or managing conflicts, but about leading by example and setting a tone that promotes under-standing and respect in all interactions.

FOUR

Emotional Intelligence

During adolescence, emotions can feel incredibly intense and overwhelming for both teens and parents. Emotional Intelligence (EI) provides a valuable set of skills to not just survive these years, but to thrive. Unlike IQ, which remains relatively stable, emotional intelligence is a dynamic set of abilities that influence how well we perceive, understand, and manage emotions in ourselves and others. These skills, including self-awareness, self-regulation, motivation, empathy, and social relationships, are essential tools that can guide your teen through the complexities of their emotional experiences. By fostering emotional intelligence, you're providing your teen with the means to navigate their emotional world, enhancing their ability to engage with others, make decisions, and pursue their goals with confidence and clarity.

Recognizing Emotions: The Basics of Emotional Intelligence

At its core, emotional intelligence is the ability to recognize, understand, and manage one's own emotions, as well as the ability to handle interpersonal relationships judiciously and empathetically. This multifaceted skill set is built on five key areas:

1. Self-awareness: The ability to recognize and understand your own emotions
2. Self-regulation: The ability to manage, control, and adapt your emotions, behavior, and responses to situations
3. Motivation: The drive to pursue goals with energy and persistence
4. Empathy: The ability to understand, recognize, and consider others' feelings, especially when making decisions
5. Social skills: The ability to manage relationships to move people in desired directions, whether in leading, negotiating, or working as part of a team

These components work synergistically to enable individuals to recognize, connect with, and learn from their own and others' emotions, which is crucial not only for personal satisfaction but also for success in various aspects of life.

To instill emotional awareness in your teen, start with simple exercises that encourage them to tune into their emotions. One effective tool is the 'Emotion Meter' exercise, where you ask your teen to imagine their emotional state as a meter running from 'very low' to 'very high'. Throughout the day, at random moments, ask them to 'check' this meter and identify what emotion they're feeling and its intensity. This exercise not only helps them become more aware of their emotional fluctuations but also helps them recognize what events or interactions trigger different emotions. Another useful practice is mindfulness meditation, focusing on breathing and bodily sensations. This can help teens become more attuned to their emotional states as they arise.

The ability to accurately identify emotions is a crucial component of emotional intelligence and can significantly improve emotional regulation. When teens can pinpoint their emotions, they're better equipped to address them effectively. For instance, recognizing the difference between feeling 'irritated' and 'angry' can lead to more appropriate responses and interactions with others. Encourage your teen to expand their emotional vocabulary beyond basic labels like "sad" or "happy." Introduce them to more nuanced terms like 'melancholy', 'anxious', or 'content', which can provide a clearer understanding of their emotional state. This practice not only improves their self-awareness but also enhances their communication with others, as they can express their feelings more accurately.

Emotional intelligence has a significant and measurable impact on success. Research shows that individuals with high EI have better mental health, job performance, and leadership skills. Studies suggest that emotional intelligence accounts for nearly 90% of what sets high performers apart from peers with similar technical skills and knowledge (Cavaness et al., 2020). When it comes to academics, teens with higher emotional intelligence are better equipped to handle academic pressures and interactions with peers and teachers; they also tend to have better conflict resolution skills and a more positive attitude towards school. Teaching your teen about the importance of emotional intelligence for real-world success can motivate them to consistently develop and apply these skills.

Exercise: Emotion Word of the Week

Objective

To expand your teen's emotional vocabulary and enhance their ability to identify and express complex emotions.

Materials

- Index cards or small pieces of paper
- Pen or marker
- Tape or magnets (for posting on the fridge)
- List of complex emotion words (provided below)

Instructions

1. At the beginning of each week, choose a new emotion word from the list.

2. Write the word and its definition on an index card or piece of paper.

3. Post the card in a visible place, such as the refrigerator or family bulletin board.

4. During a family meal or dedicated time, introduce the word:

- Read the definition aloud
- Discuss situations where someone might feel this emotion
- Share personal experiences related to the emotion, if comfortable

5. Challenge family members to use the word throughout the week when describing their feelings.

6. At the end of the week, have a brief discussion:

- How often did family members use or notice the emotion?
- Did using a more specific word help in understanding or expressing feelings?

7. Keep the used cards in a visible place to review and reinforce learning.

Sample Emotion Words:

- Melancholy
- Exhilarated
- Apprehensive
- Indignant
- Wistful

- Ambivalent
- Nostalgic
- Vulnerable
- Jubilant
- Despondent

Tips

- Encourage your teen to journal about times they experience the emotion of the week.
- Use the words in everyday conversations to model their usage.
- Consider creating a family game where points are earned for appropriately using the word of the week.

By focusing intently on developing your teen's emotional intelligence, you are setting them up not just for academic and professional success, but for a richer, more understanding, and empathetic life. These skills enable teens to navigate their emotional world with finesse, making them better students and friends, as well as, ultimately, more compassionate and effective leaders.

Managing Emotions: Strategies for Self-Regulation

In navigating the emotional complexity of the teenage years, self-regulation stands out as a critical skill that allows individuals to maintain control over their feelings and reactions, thus fostering a healthier emotional life. This ability to manage one's emotions isn't innate; rather, it's cultivated through consistent practice and the application of specific techniques that can be integrated into daily life. One of the most effective of these strategies is deep breathing, which has been shown to reduce stress and promote calmness by slowing the heart rate and providing the brain with the oxygen it needs to achieve a state of calm. Encourage your teen to practice deep breathing by inhaling slowly to a count of four, holding the breath for a count of four, then exhaling to a count of four. This technique can be particularly useful in moments of high stress or anxiety, providing them with a tool that's always available to them, no matter where they are or what situation they're in.

Mindfulness, another powerful tool for emotional regulation, involves maintaining a moment-by-moment awareness of our thoughts, feelings, bodily sensations, and surrounding environment. This practice helps teens to observe their emotions without judgment, recognizing them as temporary states that don't define their identity or capabilities. You can encourage your teen to practice mindfulness through simple exercises such as mindful walking, where the focus is on the sensation of moving and touching the ground, or mindful eating, which involves paying close attention to the eating experience and the textures, flavors, and smells of the food. These practices help to anchor them in the present moment, providing a respite from the stress of past memories or future anxieties.

Positive self-talk is another essential component of self-regulation, influencing the emotional response to various situations. Negative self-talk can spiral into emotional distress, while positive self-talk can empower and bring clarity. Encourage your teen to recognize negative thought patterns and replace them with positive affirmations. For instance, instead of thinking, "I can't handle this," they can reframe it as, "I can handle this situation step by step." Over time, this shift in internal dialogue can significantly alter their emotional landscape, changing how they perceive and react to challenges.

Maintaining emotional balance often directly correlates with how well we take care of our physical health. Regular exercise, adequate sleep, and healthy eating habits are fundamental elements that contribute significantly to emotional well-being. Physical activity, for instance, isn't just about staying in shape; it's a powerful mood enhancer and anxiety reducer. Encourage your teen to find a form of exercise they enjoy, whether it's dancing, skateboarding, or playing soccer. The key is consistency and enjoyment, which will make it more likely that they'll stick with it.

Sleep also plays a crucial role in emotional regulation. Lack of sleep can make teens more prone to emotional instability, irritability, and stress. Help your teen establish a healthy sleep routine by encouraging a consistent bedtime and creating a pre-sleep ritual that avoids screens and incorporates calming activities like reading or listening to soothing music. Dietary habits also influence mood and energy levels. Diets high in processed foods and sugars can exacerbate feelings of lethargy and depression, while a balanced diet rich in vegetables, fruits, and whole grains can improve energy and emotional resilience. Discuss these connections with your teen and involve them in making better food choices; perhaps plan and cook meals together to make this practice more engaging and educational.

Helping your teen set and maintain healthy emotional boundaries is crucial for their self-esteem and emotional well-being. These boundaries help them define what they're comfortable with and how they want to be treated by others. Encourage your teen to listen to their feelings and recognize when a situation or person is making them uncomfortable. Discuss scenarios where they might need to assert their boundaries, such as when someone asks them to do something they're not comfortable with or when they need personal space. Role-playing can be a useful tool here, helping them practice how to assert themselves in a respectful and confident manner. It's important they understand that saying no is a right, not a privilege, and that setting boundaries is a sign of self-respect, not selfishness.

The ability to pause and choose how to respond to a situation is a sophisticated skill that lies at the heart of emotional intelligence. This practice involves shifting from being reactive—acting on immediate emotional impulses—to being responsive—taking a moment to consider the best course of action. Encourage your teen to develop the habit of pausing when they feel emotionally triggered. This pause can be as simple as taking three deep breaths to give them time to consider how best to respond. During this time, they can evaluate whether their immediate reaction is likely to lead to a positive outcome or whether there might be a better way to handle the situation. This practice not only prevents regrettable actions made in the heat of the moment but also empowers your teen to approach challenges in a more thoughtful and effective manner.

By incorporating these strategies and practices into their daily life, your teen can develop powerful self-regulation skills that will serve them well through adolescence and beyond. These skills are fundamental to self-mastery, fostering a sense of control and resilience that will help them navigate the complex emotional landscapes of their teenage years and prepare them for the adult world.

Empathy: Walking in Someone Else's Shoes

As we discussed earlier in Chapter 3, empathy is a crucial skill for effective communication and building relationships. In the context of emotional intelligence, empathy takes on an even more significant role. It's not just about understanding others' feelings, but also using that understanding to navigate social situations more effectively.

Empathy and active listening, which we explored in depth previously, are fundamental to developing high emotional intelligence. They allow teens to pick up on subtle emotional cues, respond appropriately to others' feelings, and build stronger, more meaningful connections. By honing these skills, teens can enhance their overall emotional intelligence, leading to better social outcomes and personal growth.

The impact of empathy on relationships cannot be overstated. It serves as a powerful bridge between individuals, fostering a culture of trust and openness. When your teen learns to empathize, they're not just understanding another person's situation; they're also validating their feelings. This validation can be incredibly affirming, strengthening the bonds between individuals. It encourages a reciprocal flow of openness and trust that can transform relationships. For instance, when a friend or family member is going through a difficult time, your teen's ability to empathize allows them to offer genuine support and understanding, which can be crucial for the other person's emotional well-being. In turn, this builds a relationship based on mutual respect and understanding, qualities that are essential for lasting connections.

To enhance empathy, consider incorporating practices into your teen's routine that foster perspective-taking and emotional understanding. Volunteer work is an excellent way for teens to experience different situations that challenge their viewpoints and evoke empathy. Whether it's helping at a local shelter, assisting in community clean-up efforts, or participating in programs for underprivileged groups, these activities can open their eyes to the realities of different lives. Such experiences not only cultivate a deeper understanding of societal issues but also inspire a profound sense of empathy for individuals from diverse backgrounds.

Exercise: Empathy Through Community Engagement

Objective

To develop empathy and broaden perspectives through hands-on volunteer experiences.

Materials

- List of local volunteer opportunities
- Calendar for planning
- Journal or notebook

Instructions

1. Research and Exploration (1-2 weeks):

- Together with your teen, research local volunteer opportunities.

- Look for diverse options such as:

  - Animal shelters
  - Food banks
  - Community clean-up projects
  - Senior centers
  - Youth mentoring programs
  - Homeless shelters

2. Selection and Planning:

- Have your teen choose 2-3 different volunteer activities.
- Schedule these activities over the course of 1-3 months.
- Discuss expectations and any concerns before each activity.

3. Engagement:

- Participate in the chosen volunteer activities together.
- Encourage your teen to interact with people they meet and ask questions.

4. Reflection: After each volunteer experience, engage in a reflection session:

- What surprised you about this experience?
- How did it make you feel?
- Did you meet anyone whose story impacted you? How?
- How has this changed your perspective on [relevant issue]?

5. Journaling:

- Have your teen write about their experiences in a journal.
- Prompt them to describe not just what they did, but how it affected them emotionally.

6. Follow-up Discussion:

- After completing all planned activities, have a family discussion about the overall experience.
- Explore how these experiences have influenced your teen's understanding of others and their empathy levels.

7. Continued Engagement:

- Based on your teen's interests and reflections, consider committing to regular volunteer work in one area.

Tips

- Lead by example; share your own reflections and emotional responses.
- Encourage your teen to step out of their comfort zone, but be supportive if they find certain experiences challenging.
- Use these experiences as springboards for discussions about social issues, inequality, and the importance of community support.

Additionally, exploring diverse perspectives is another enriching exercise. This can be achieved through family discussions about current events, books, or movies that explore complex human emotions and situations. Encourage your teen to share their thoughts and feelings about the characters or situations, and explore how they might feel in similar circumstances. These conversations can be instrumental in fostering a well-rounded, empathetic approach to differing viewpoints.

In the digital world, empathy presents unique challenges. Often, the nuances of face-to-face interaction, such as tone of voice and body language, are lost in online communication, making it harder to perceive and convey empathy. This can lead to misunderstandings or a perceived lack of concern. To help your teen navigate these challenges, discuss the importance of being mindful of how their words might be interpreted without the benefit of non-verbal cues. Encourage them to use empathetic language that reflects thoughtfulness and understanding, as well as to ask clarifying questions to ensure they've accurately perceived others' messages. Additionally, practicing empathy online can involve acknowledging others' emotions explicitly and offering support through thoughtful comments or messages. These practices can make a significant difference in fostering meaningful connections, even through digital mediums. Importantly, developing these digital empathy skills directly enhances emotional intelligence by improving one's ability to recognize, understand, and respond to emotions in various contexts, building upon the foundational empathy concepts discussed in Chapter 3.

By teaching your teen to cultivate empathy, both offline and online, you equip them with the ability to understand and connect with others deeply, enhancing their interpersonal relationships and boosting their emotional intelligence. This skill set not only aids their personal and social interactions but also prepares them to engage with the world from a more compassionate and comprehensive perspective.

Resilience: Bouncing Back from Social Setbacks

Resilience, often envisioned as the psychological armor against the slings and arrows of outrageous fortune, is fundamentally about more than just enduring; it's about adapting and thriving in the face of adversity. In the context of social interactions, particularly during the tumultuous years of adolescence, resilience is the ability to recover from setbacks, learn from failure, and move forward with a more refined understanding and renewed vigor. This capacity is especially critical for teenagers, who often face a myriad of social challenges, from navigating complex friendship dynamics to dealing with rejection or bullying. Understanding and cultivating resilience can transform these potentially traumatic experiences into powerful opportunities for growth and learning.

Fostering a resilient mindset is a proactive approach that involves reframing challenges as catalysts for growth. This mindset, rooted in what psychologist Carol Dweck terms a "growth mindset," contrasts sharply with a "fixed mindset," which views abilities and intelligence as static and sees challenges as threats (Dweck, 2012). Encourage your teen to view setbacks as opportunities to expand their skills and gain new insights. For example, if they face rejection from a group, rather than interpreting it as a personal failure, guide them to see it as a chance to explore new social circles and develop broader interests. This perspective not only mitigates the pain associated with the experience but also propels them towards self-discovery and personal growth.

To nurture this mindset, regular discussions about the nature of learning and growth can be incredibly beneficial. Highlight stories of individuals who have overcome significant social setbacks to achieve remarkable personal and professional success. These narratives can serve as powerful reminders that current difficulties do not define future outcomes, and that persistence and resilience can lead to unexpected and fulfilling paths. Additionally, focusing on intrinsic rather than extrinsic rewards can reinforce the value of self-improvement. Encourage your teen to set goals related to acquiring new skills or expanding knowledge in areas of interest, rather than goals solely tied to social acceptance or status. This shift in focus can lessen the sting of social challenges and reframe their purpose from gaining external validation to enhancing personal growth.

Exercise: Building Your Personal Resilience Toolkit

Objective

To create a personalized set of coping strategies for your teen to manage stress, disappointment, and failure.

Materials

- Notebook or journal
- Pens or pencils
- Art supplies (optional)
- Yoga mat or comfortable space for relaxation exercises

Instructions

1. Journaling for Reflection (15-20 minutes daily)

- Dedicate a notebook specifically for resilience journaling.
- Each day, have your teen write about:
- A challenge they faced
- How they felt during and after
- What they learned from the experience
- How they might apply this lesson in the future
- At the end of each week, sit with your teen and review their entries to identify patterns in their responses to challenges.

2. Stress-Relief Activity Menu (One-time setup, then daily practice)

- Sit down with your teen and create a list of 5-10 activities that help them relax and reduce stress. Examples might include:

  - Deep breathing exercises
  - Drawing or coloring
  - Listening to calming music

- Taking a nature walk
- Practicing yoga or stretching

- Encourage your teen to engage in at least one of these activities daily, especially during stressful times. Consider joining them occasionally to model the importance of stress management.

3. Positive Affirmation Creation (Weekly)

- Each week, work with your teen to create a new positive affirmation based on a challenge they're facing or a strength they want to reinforce.
- Help them write it down and place it somewhere visible in their room.
- Encourage them to repeat the affirmation to themselves several times a day, especially when feeling stressed or discouraged.

4. Problem-Solving Practice (As needed)

When your teen faces a difficult situation, guide them through these steps: a) Help them write down the problem. b) Brainstorm together to list at least three possible solutions. c) Discuss the pros and cons of each solution. d) Support them in choosing one to implement. e) After implementing, reflect together on the outcome and encourage them to journal about it.

5. Gratitude Log (Daily)

- Introduce the concept of a gratitude journal to your teen.
- Encourage them to write down three things they're grateful for each day.
- Challenge them to find new things to appreciate, especially on difficult days.

- Consider sharing your own gratitudes at dinner time to make it a family activity.

6. Resilience Role Model Research (Monthly)

- Suggest that your teen research someone who has shown great resilience in the face of adversity.
- Ask them to write a short summary of the person's story and what they find inspiring about their resilience.
- Discuss their findings together, drawing parallels to your teen's life where appropriate.

7. Toolkit Review and Update (Monthly)

- At the end of each month, review your teen's journal entries and activities together.
- Discuss what strategies worked best for them.
- Help them adjust their toolkit as needed, adding new techniques or modifying existing ones.

Remember to approach these activities with patience and support. Your involvement can greatly enhance your teen's resilience-building journey and strengthen your relationship.

The resilience toolkit contains essential tools for managing particularly difficult times for handling stress, disappointment, and failure. Techniques such as journaling can provide a safe outlet for emotional expression and reflection. Encourage your teen to write about their experiences and feelings, focusing on what they learned from each situation and how they can apply these lessons in the future. This practice aids in processing emotions and, moreover, in identifying patterns in how they respond to challenges, which can be insightful for personal growth. Additionally, engaging in activities that promote relaxation and stress relief, such as yoga or creative arts, can provide a healthy escape from social stressors, offering space and energy to approach problems with a clearer mind.

Learning from failure is perhaps the most crucial aspect of developing resilience. It involves shifting the narrative from viewing failure as a negative endpoint to seeing it as an essential part of the growth process. This shift requires a supportive environment where mistakes are tolerated, as well as regular steps in the direction of learning and adapting. When your teen experiences a social setback, help them analyze the situation to understand what factors were within their control and what lessons could be gleaned. Was it a matter of misaligned expectations, miscommunications, or perhaps a need for better conflict resolution skills? Each of these revelations can guide them to specific areas for improvement. Furthermore, encourage them to set up small, manageable experiments in social settings to test new ways of interacting or coping with social pressure. This approach not only builds resilience but also improves their social skills through practical experience.

These skills help your teen not just bounce back from social setbacks but leap forward, equipped with deeper insights, refined skills, and a resilient mindset. This empowerment enables them to navigate their social world with confidence, viewing each challenge as a stepping stone to greater personal and social competence. As they continue to grow and face new challenges, the resilience they develop now will serve as a core strength, supporting their journey towards becoming well-rounded, emotionally intelligent adults.

Celebrating Emotional Successes: Recognizing Growth

Recognizing and celebrating each forward step in the ongoing development of your teen's emotional intelligence is crucial in reinforcing their growth and motivation. Just as we track academic progress with grades and comments, marking emotional progress requires a systematic yet personal approach. Encouraging your teen to keep an emotional growth journal can be an effective way to do this. In this journal, they can record daily or weekly entries about situations that evoked strong emotions, their responses, and reflections on how they handled those feelings. Over time, this journal becomes a valuable tool for your teen to see their progress in handling complex emotions, increasing self-awareness, and improving their relationships. It's not just about recording events; it's about reflecting on them, which deepens their understanding and investment in their emotional journey.

The act of tracking these emotional milestones should be complemented by positive reinforcement, a powerful motivator that can transform the challenging path of emotional growth into an encouraging and rewarding experience. Celebrate these achievements, no matter how small they may seem. Did your teen handle a previously triggering situation with grace? Did they show remarkable empathy in a complex social interaction? Acknowledge these victories with sincerity and enthusiasm. You might set up a family dinner to celebrate these wins, or perhaps a special outing. What matters is that the celebration is tangible and meaningful to your teen, reinforcing their positive behaviors and encouraging them to continue developing their emotional skills.

Beyond the immediate family, the impact of role models who embody strong emotional intelligence can be profoundly inspiring for teenagers. Share stories of notable figures who have demonstrated exceptional emotional intelligence, such as Malala Yousafzai's empathy and resilience or Nelson Mandela's forgiveness and leadership. Discuss how these figures dealt with internal struggles, as well as what your teen could learn from their experiences. You can also highlight role models within your own community—teachers, family friends, or leaders who embody emotional intelligence. If possible, facilitate connections where your teen can learn directly from these role models, providing them with real-life examples of how emotional intelligence can be a powerful tool for personal and professional success.

Creating a family culture of emotional support is the foundation for nurturing your teen's emotional intelligence. This involves more than occasional discussions or scattered encouragement; it's about weaving emotional growth into the daily fabric of family life. Make it a habit to discuss emotions openly and without judgment, allowing each family member to express how they feel about various life situations. Encourage empathy by asking family members to consider each other's perspectives during these discussions. Additionally, foster an environment where emotional expressions, whether of joy, frustration, or sadness, are met with support and understanding rather than dismissal. This supportive atmosphere not only enhances each family member's emotional intelligence but also strengthens the emotional bonds within the family, creating a shared sense of understanding and respect that transcends the minutiae of daily interactions.

By integrating these practices into your daily life, you help create a nurturing environment that celebrates emotional growth, equipping your teen with the confidence and skills to continue their development. This ongoing recognition and support not only boost their self-esteem but also reinforce the importance of emotional intelligence in achieving a balanced and fulfilling life.

Exercise: Emotion Exploration Workshop

Objective

To enhance emotional awareness and expression through creative and interactive exercises.

Materials

- Large sheets of paper or poster board
- Colored markers, crayons, or paint
- Emotion cards (with various emotion words written on them)
- Soft background music (optional)

Instructions

1. Emotion Mapping (20 minutes):

- Give each participant a large sheet of paper and coloring materials.
- Ask them to draw an outline of a human body.
- Using the emotion cards as inspiration, have them color or draw where they feel different emotions in their body (e.g., anger might be red in the chest, joy could be yellow in the stomach).
- Discuss the completed emotion maps, comparing similarities and differences.

2. Emotion Charades (15 minutes):

- Take turns drawing emotion cards and acting out the emotion without words.
- Others guess the emotion being portrayed.
- After guessing, discuss how the emotion was expressed and recognized.

3. Emotional Storytelling (20 minutes):

- In pairs (teen and adult), create a short story incorporating at least three emotions from the emotion cards.
- Share the stories with the group, emphasizing how the emotions influenced the characters' actions and decisions.

4. Reflection and Discussion (15 minutes):

- Discuss what participants learned about emotions during the activities.
- Share any surprises or insights about how emotions are experienced and expressed.

- Talk about how understanding emotions can improve communication and relationships.

5. Emotion Action Plan (10 minutes):

- Each participant creates a personal action plan for practicing emotional awareness in the coming week.
- Share these plans and commit to checking in with each other about progress.

This activity workshop provides a fun, interactive way for teens and adults to explore emotions together, fostering deeper understanding and open communication about emotional experiences.

As we wrap up this chapter on emotional intelligence, your focus should center on the profound impact that recognizing, tracking, and celebrating emotional growth can have on your teen's development. These practices are not just about fostering emotional intelligence, but about creating a supportive environment that encourages continuous learning and emotional well-being. As we move forward, the focus will shift from internal growth to external expressions, exploring how these emotional skills manifest in personal relationships and social interactions, setting the stage for the next chapter on building effective and resilient personal connections. Remember, the journey of emotional intelligence is ongoing, and each step your teen takes is a victory worth acknowledging and celebrating.

Sharing the Power of Building Social Skills

Earlier in this book, we explored the profound impact of the digital age on teen social interactions. We discussed how social media and online communication have become the new norm, reshaping how teens connect, express themselves, and build relationships. The digital landscape is just the tip of the iceberg. We've also explored the challenges of social anxiety, the importance of emotional intelligence, and the power of effective communication. These are all crucial components of social resilience, but so too is understanding how to navigate the complex digital social world our teens inhabit.

Building social skills in the digital age isn't about putting on a brave face behind a screen or hiding what we feel in cryptic posts. Quite the opposite. It's about learning to express emotions authentically online and offline, understanding that challenges in both realms are opportunities for growth, and developing the resilience to push through the inevitable awkward moments and missteps.

I hope that by this stage in your reading, you've seen how the strategies in this book can lead to positive choices such as encouraging open dialogue, setting healthy boundaries, and fostering independence while offering support. If the insights and activities in this book have made a difference in your approach to supporting your teen's social development, then you're in the perfect position to help other parents and teens.

By leaving a review on Amazon, you'll help other readers discover the key steps they need to take to support their teens in developing crucial social skills in the digital age.

Share your opinion of this book and a little bit about your own experiences applying its strategies. One of the most powerful ways to reinforce your own learning is to help others understand these important concepts.

Please scan the QR code to leave a review.

Thank you for your support. Together, we can shine a light on the transformative power of understanding and nurturing teen social skills in our rapidly changing world.

FIVE

Building Confidence and Self-Esteem

As parents, perhaps the most extraordinary gift you can offer your teens is the power of confidence—a robust sense of self-worth that transcends the fleeting approval of peers and the ephemeral highs of social media. This chapter delves into the bedrock of confidence, exploring how core beliefs about ourselves shape interactions and perceptions, both internally and externally. Self-esteem isn't just about feeling good; it's about recognizing and embracing one's capabilities and worth, even in the face of challenges and setbacks. This core strength enables teens to navigate life's complexities with resilience and grace.

The Confidence Foundation: Building Self-Worth

The journey to solid self-esteem often begins with recognizing and celebrating one's accomplishments, no matter how small. As a parent, you play a crucial role in helping your teens discover and leverage their strengths. Encourage your teens to engage in activities that not only interest them but also challenge their abilities. Whether it's sports, the arts, coding, or volunteer work, active participation and gradual mastery provide tangible evidence of their capabilities, fostering pride. Each achievement builds upon their self-confidence, reinforcing their view of themselves as competent and capable individuals. It's important to acknowledge these achievements—not just the outcomes but also the effort and progress. This recognition anchors their self-worth beyond external validation, rooting their sense of self-value in something more substantial and enduring than transient external approval.

The internal narrative teens have about themselves shapes their self-image and, by extension, confidence. Positive affirmations are a powerful tool for reshaping this narrative. These are positive, first-person statements that are repeated regularly and reflect the qualities or goals teens aspire to. For instance, affirmations like "I am capable of achieving my goals," "I deserve respect from others and myself," or "I handle challenges with courage and grace" help to internalize these positive beliefs, countering the negative self-talk that can erode confidence. Encourage your teen to create a list of personal affirmations that resonate with their aspirations and challenges. Placing these affirmations in visible places—like mirrors, study areas, or journals—can serve as constant reminders of their inherent worth and strengths, silently reinforcing a positive self-image throughout the day.

Your role in nurturing your teen's self-esteem is paramount. Through your words, actions, and reactions, you can profoundly influence how your teen perceives and feels about themselves. It starts with demonstrating unconditional love and acceptance, conveying to your teen that they are valued primarily for being themselves, not just for their achievements or compliance. Rather than solely praising their successes, consistently express admiration for their effort and resilience. For example, commend them for working hard on a test, even if the grade wasn't perfect, or for standing up for a friend, highlighting the character shown rather than the outcome. Such encouragement helps teens internalize a sense of self-worth that's stable and independent of external accomplishments or others' opinions.

In today's digital age, teens are bombarded with curated glimpses into others' lives, often leading to unfavorable comparisons that can distort self-images and erode confidence. Discuss with your teen the skewed reality of social media, where individuals often showcase enhanced, filtered versions of their lives. Encourage them to be critical consumers of the content they consume, prompting them to question the reality behind the idealized images. Help them focus on their own journey and personal growth rather than comparing themselves to others. Activities like a "social media detox," where they take breaks from social media, can help reduce the impact of these comparisons by refocusing on offline activities that contribute to a sense of real accomplishment and joy. These discussions and activities help teens build a healthier self-image and value their own authentic experiences and achievements, reducing the insecurity that often comes from online comparisons.

Exercise: Building a Confidence Vision Board

Objective

To create a visual representation of your teen's strengths, goals, and positive self-image, reinforcing their self-esteem and confidence.

Materials

- Large poster board or cork board
- Magazines, newspapers, or printed images
- Scissors
- Glue or pushpins
- Markers or colored pens
- Small notepad and pen for journaling

Instructions

1. Strength Identification (15 minutes):

   - Have your teen write down 5-10 personal strengths or qualities they admire about themselves.
   - Encourage them to think about compliments they've received or challenges they've overcome.

2. Goal Setting (15 minutes):

   - Ask your teen to write down 3-5 social or personal goals they'd like to achieve.
   - Ensure these goals are specific and achievable.

3. Positive Affirmations (10 minutes):

   - Help your teen create 3-5 positive affirmations that resonate with them.
   - Examples: "I am capable of making new friends," "I handle challenges with courage."

4. Image Collection (20 minutes):

   - Have your teen look through magazines or online images to find pictures that represent their strengths, goals, and positive self-image.
   - Encourage them to also find images of role models or inspirational quotes.

5. Vision Board Creation (30 minutes):

   - Guide your teen in arranging and gluing the images, strengths, goals, and affirmations on the board.
   - Encourage creativity in the layout and design.

6. Reflection and Sharing (15 minutes):

- Ask your teen to explain their vision board to you.
- Discuss how each element contributes to their confidence and self-esteem.

7. Display and Daily Reflection:

- Place the vision board where your teen can see it daily.
- Encourage a brief daily journaling session where they reflect on one element of their board and how it relates to their day.

8. Monthly Review:

- Schedule a monthly check-in to discuss the vision board.
- Update or add to the board as your teen grows and achieves goals.

You are laying a strong foundation of confidence that will support your teen through the challenges and triumphs of their formative years. This foundation not only enhances their current well-being but also equips them with the self-assurance to face the world with confidence and resilience, embracing opportunities to grow and thrive.

Positive Self-Talk: Changing the Inner Dialogue

The conversations that occur within the quiet confines of our minds are just as critical as the ones we have with the world. For teenagers, these internal dialogues can often spiral into negative self-talk, undermining confidence and fostering self-doubt. You, as a parent, can play a pivotal role in helping your teen recognize and reshape these inner narratives into a source of strength and self-assurance.

The first step in this transformative process is helping your teen become aware of their self-talk. Negative or self-deprecating thoughts often operate just below the surface of consciousness, influencing emotions and behaviors without ever being fully recognized. These might manifest as beliefs like "I'm not good enough," "I can't do this," or "Everyone is better than me," which can erode self-esteem over time. Encourage your teen to tune into these thoughts, perhaps during moments of stress or frustration, and to capture them in writing. This act of identification is powerful; it externalizes thoughts and makes them easier to address.

Once these thoughts are recognized, the next step is to challenge and reframe them into more positive and empowering narratives. This process, often referred to as cognitive restructuring, involves questioning the validity of negative thoughts and replacing them with more constructive ones. For example, the thought "I always mess up" can be challenged with "Everyone makes mistakes; I can learn from this." Or, "I'm not good at this" can be reframed to "I'm not good at this yet, but I can improve with practice." These revised thoughts encourage a mindset of growth and possibility rather than one of limitation and defeat. Encouraging your teen to practice this type of reframing can transform a moment of self-doubt into an opportunity for growth and self-compassion.

Keeping a self-talk journal can be incredibly helpful during this process. This journal should be a dedicated space where your teen can record negative thoughts that arise along with their more positive reframing. This not only helps in tracking patterns of negative thinking but also provides a tangible method for practicing and reinforcing positive self-talk. Over time, this journal can become a personal testament to your teen's ability to reshape their thinking, bolster their confidence, and provide a clear record of personal growth.

The overarching power of mindset in this journey cannot be overstated. The concept of a growth mindset posits that our fundamental qualities are things we can cultivate through our efforts. This belief is central to building genuine self-confidence, as it shifts the focus from achieving to improving oneself. As we reviewed in Chapter 4 when discussing resilience, understanding the difference between growth and fixed mindsets is crucial not only for resilience but also for developing increased self-esteem and confidence.

Unlike a fixed mindset, which views abilities and intelligence as static, a growth mindset thrives on challenge and sees failure not as evidence of unintelligence but as a springboard for growth and stretching our existing abilities. Fundamentally, this mindset changes how teens view challenges and setbacks, imbuing them with a sense of resilience and an understanding that abilities can be developed through dedication and hard work.

Explaining and modeling this mindset can have a profound impact on how your teen talks to themselves about their capabilities and challenges. It reinforces their belief that they are in control of their own abilities and that with effort, strategy, and input from others, they can grow and succeed.

By guiding your teen through these strategies—helping them recognize and reframe their inner dialogues, keeping a journal of their cognitive restructuring, and fostering a growth mindset—you empower them to cultivate a self-supportive and resilient inner narrative. These skills not only enhance their self-esteem but also equip them with the mental tools to face life's challenges from a place of strength and optimism.

Overcoming the Fear of Rejection: Strategies for Resilience

Understanding the nuanced nature of rejection is crucial to helping your teen navigate their social landscape more confidently. Rejection, at its core, taps into some of our most primal fears—those of abandonment and isolation that trace back to our early ancestors, for whom exclusion from the group could have dire consequences. Today, while the stakes might not be survival, the emotional impact of rejection retains its potency. It's important to teach your teen that this fear isn't just normal; it's universal. Discussing the evolutionary roots of this fear can provide them with a broader perspective, helping them understand that their feelings of distress are part of a deeply ingrained human experience. This understanding can often be the first step in mitigating the sting of rejection, as it allows teens to feel less isolated in their experiences, fostering a sense of shared human vulnerability.

Rejection often feels deeply personal, like a direct assessment of one's essence or worth. As such, teaching teens to depersonalize rejection is essential to helping them develop resilience. It's crucial to convey that rejection can be caused by a multitude of factors that have nothing to do with their personal qualities or worth. For instance, a friend might decline an invitation not because they dislike the person inviting them, but because they have other commitments or are dealing with personal issues. Encourage your teen to consider these external factors, which often play a significant role in rejection. This shift in perspective can significantly alleviate the personal blame and shame that often accompany rejection. Framing rejection as a redirection rather than a personal failure can also be helpful. This viewpoint allows each rejection to be an opportunity to explore new avenues or relationships that might be more aligned with their values and interests.

Building emotional resilience against rejection requires more than just understanding and perspective; it necessitates active practice and skill development. One effective practice is the use of visualization techniques, where your teen can imagine facing a rejection scenario and handling it calmly and constructively. Guide them through envisioning the situation in detail—the setting, the people involved, what is said—and how they can respond in a way that maintains their self-esteem and dignity. Another powerful strategy is resilience training through exposure, which involves encouraging your teen to put themselves in low-risk social situations where rejection might occur, such as joining a new club or volunteering at a new organization. These controlled exposures can desensitize them to the fear of rejection and help them develop coping strategies in a safe environment.

Furthermore, establishing techniques like deep breathing, mindfulness, or focusing on physical sensations can help manage the immediate emotional turmoil that rejection can trigger. These techniques provide practical tools that your teen can use to regain their emotional balance in the face of rejection.

Encouraging reflection on past rejections is another valuable strategy for learning and growth. This reflection can be done through conversations or journaling, where your teen can explore what they learned from the experience, how they coped, and what they might do differently in the future. This process not only helps in processing the emotions associated with rejection but also transforms the experience from a purely negative event into a learning opportunity. Ask your teen questions like, "What did this experience teach you about your needs and boundaries?" or "How might you use this experience to strengthen your future interactions?" These reflections can foster a more proactive and empowered approach to social challenges, helping your teen view rejection as a normal part of life that holds valuable lessons and opportunities for self-improvement.

By incorporating these discussions, practices, and exercises into your parenting approach, you are providing your teen with tools not just to cope with rejection but to emerge from it stronger and more resilient. This skill set is invaluable, as it not only enhances their current well-being and social interactions but also lays the groundwork for handling the inevitable challenges of life with confidence and poise.

Role Models and Mentors: Finding Inspiration

In the complex tapestry of adolescent development, the threads woven by role models and mentors hold a distinct place, providing guidance, inspiration, and practical examples of the kind of person a teen might aspire to become. Identifying and engaging with role models can significantly shape your teen's aspirations and behaviors, offering them tangible examples of success and the qualities needed to achieve it. Facilitating the identification of these figures is crucial for a parent. Encourage your teen to look for qualities that resonate with their own aspirations, whether in public figures, community leaders, teachers, or even within the family. This process involves more than just admiring someone's achievements; it's about recognizing the qualities that helped them succeed, such as perseverance, integrity, empathy, and resilience.

Discussing the value of mentorship can have a profound impact on your teen's perspective on growth and development. Mentors provide more than just guidance; they offer support, wisdom, and a framework within which your teen can explore their identity and capabilities. A mentor acts as a sounding board and role model in real-time, offering both aspirational and practical insights. For instance, a coach or music teacher can guide your teen in developing specific skills as well as imparting life lessons like teamwork, discipline, and the importance of practice. Encourage your teen to actively seek out mentor relationships, whether through school programs, clubs, or community organizations. These relationships can provide them with a safe space to explore new ideas and challenges, bolstered by the support and guidance of someone they trust and respect.

Learning from the experiences of role models can also be incredibly inspiring. Encourage your teen to read biographies or watch documentaries about individuals they admire. This exploration can provide insight into the challenges these figures faced and how they overcame them. It's important for teens to understand that all successes come with trials and failures, and that resilience and persistence are often the keys to achieving one's goals. These stories can make the journey of their role models feel more relatable and attainable, reinforcing the idea that they, too, can achieve great things if they commit to their goals and learn from their setbacks.

Becoming a role model is an empowering goal for teens. It encourages them to embody the qualities they admire in others and act in ways that can positively influence those around them. Discuss with your teen how they can be a role model to younger siblings, peers, or community members. This could involve taking on leadership roles in school activities, volunteering for community service, or simply being a supportive friend. Encourage them to consider how their actions and choices can inspire others, emphasizing that they have the power to make a positive impact. This perspective can significantly enhance their self-esteem and sense of responsibility as they recognize the value and influence of their actions within their peer groups and communities.

By incorporating these elements—identifying role models, engaging with mentors, learning from others' experiences, and becoming a role model themselves—your teen is equipped not only to aspire to greater heights but also to lay a strong foundation for their personal and social development. This approach enhances their current adolescent experience and prepares them for future roles in society where they can continue to inspire and lead by example.

Setting and Achieving Social Goals: Small Wins Matter

Setting achievable goals plays a crucial role in enhancing your teen's social skills and helping them become confident and socially competent individuals. This process starts with helping them set realistic social goals—targets that are specific, attainable, and tailored to their personal growth needs. This could include initiating conversations with peers, joining a club or group, or simply trying to spend more time with friends outside of school. The key here is to ensure that these goals are small enough to be comfortable, yet challenging enough to push their boundaries. For instance, if your teen is naturally introverted, a goal might be to initiate a conversation with one new person each week. This gradual approach helps build confidence without overwhelming them with too-high expectations. It's important to work closely with your teen to establish these goals and involve them actively in the process, so they feel ownership and responsibility for their social growth.

As these goals are set, the importance of recognizing and celebrating each achievement along the way cannot be overstated. Every small victory is a building block in the larger structure of self-confidence and social competence. Celebrate these milestones, whether it's your teen making a new friend, contributing to a group project, or attending a gathering they were initially anxious about. These celebrations can be simple acknowledgments or small rewards that recognize their effort and accomplishment. This practice not only reinforces positive behaviors but also motivates your teen, encouraging them to continue stepping out of their comfort zone. Maintaining an atmosphere of positivity and encouragement and focusing on their progress rather than perfection is key. This supportive environment is crucial in helping them persevere through social challenges and setbacks.

Introducing the concept of an accountability partner can further enhance your teen's commitment to their social goals. This partner could be a friend, a sibling, or even a parent—someone who checks in on their progress regularly, offers moral support, and keeps them motivated. This relationship adds a layer of accountability and support, making the goal-setting process more dynamic and interactive. For teenagers, knowing someone else is rooting for their success and aware of their objectives can be a powerful motivator. It also adds a social element to their goal achievements, making the process more enjoyable and less daunting. Encourage your teen to choose someone they trust and feel comfortable with as their accountability partner, and discuss how this partnership can help them move towards their social goals.

Flexibility in goal setting is another crucial aspect, as it allows for adjustments based on your teen's experiences and growth. As they progress, some goals may become too easy, while others might prove too ambitious. It's important to periodically review these goals with your teen, discussing what's working and what isn't. This review can be a regular part of the conversation with their accountability partner, where they can reflect on their progress and determine if any goals need to be adjusted. For example, if your teen has become comfortable initiating conversations with new people, they might shift their focus towards deepening existing relationships or participating in more public speaking opportunities. This flexibility keeps the goals relevant and challenging, but it also teaches your teen an important life skill: the ability to evaluate and adjust their strategies in various aspects of life based on ongoing results and changing circumstances.

Through these strategies—setting realistic goals, celebrating small victories, having accountability partners, and maintaining flexibility in their objectives—you are helping to scaffold your teen's social development in a structured yet adaptable way. This approach not only enhances their current social skills but also sets a pattern of continuous improvement and adaptation that they can apply throughout their lives in various settings beyond the social domain.

Exercise: Social Goal-Setting Workshop

Objective

To create and implement a personalized social goal plan for both teen and parent.

Materials

- Notebook or journal for each participant
- Pens or pencils
- Calendar or planner
- Stickers or small rewards for goal achievements

Instructions

1. Goal Brainstorming (15 minutes):

- Both teen and parent individually write down 3-5 social goals they'd like to achieve.
- Goals should be specific, measurable, achievable, relevant, and time-bound (SMART).

2. Goal Sharing and Refinement (20 minutes):

- Discuss each other's goals.
- Help refine goals to ensure they're realistic and challenging.
- Select 1-2 primary goals for each person to focus on.

3. Action Plan Creation (20 minutes):

- For each primary goal, create a step-by-step action plan.
- Break down larger goals into smaller, weekly objectives.
- Identify potential obstacles and strategies to overcome them.

4. Accountability System (10 minutes):

- Decide on check-in frequency (e.g., weekly) and method (e.g., Sunday evening discussions).
- Create a simple tracking system in the notebook or planner.
- Agree on how to celebrate small victories (e.g., special treat, family movie night).

5. First Step Commitment (5 minutes):

- Each person commits to taking one small action toward their goal within the next 24 hours.
- Write down this commitment and share it aloud.

6. Ongoing Process:

- Hold regular check-ins as agreed.
- Adjust goals and strategies as needed.
- Celebrate achievements together.
- After a month, review overall progress and set new goals if needed.

This activity fosters a collaborative approach to social growth, allowing both parent and teen to work on personal goals while supporting each other. It demonstrates that social skill development is a lifelong process and helps strengthen the parent-teen relationship through shared goal-setting and achievement.

As we conclude this chapter on building confidence and self-esteem, remember the powerful role of goal-setting in shaping your teen's growth. Setting and achieving social goals provides tangible evidence of progress, reinforcing self-confidence and social competence. These small wins accumulate, creating a positive cycle of growth and achievement. Moving forward, the next chapter will explore navigating the social landscape, where these lessons in confidence and self-esteem will be put into practice, helping your teen interact with the world with assurance and grace.

Navigating the Social Landscape

I magine that your teen stands at the edge of a maze. Each path represents a different social choice, each turn a potential shift in their journey of self-discovery. The walls of this maze aren't made of stone or hedge; they're constructed from the expectations, pressures, and influences of peers. Welcome to the social landscape of adolescence—a terrain as challenging as it is transformative.

As parents, we often wish we could hand our teens a map to navigate this complex world. But the truth is, there is no one-size-fits-all guide. Instead, what we can offer is a compass—a set of tools and strategies to help them find their way while staying true to themselves. This chapter is about equipping your teen with that compass, helping them understand the forces at play in their social world, and empowering them to make choices that align with their values and nurture their authentic selves.

Understanding Peer Pressure: Strategies to Stand Strong

Let's start a topic that affects almost all teens: peer pressure. It's a force as old as socializing itself, yet it takes on new dimensions in the teenage years. Peer pressure isn't always the dramatic, after-school special scenario we might imagine. More often, it's a subtle current, pushing and pulling our teens in ways they might not even recognize.

Defining peer pressure is the first step in understanding its impact. It's not just about being explicitly pressured to try drugs or skip class. Peer pressure is the influence that a group or individual has on someone to conform to certain behaviors, dress codes, or attitudes. It can be as subtle as the unspoken expectation to have the latest smartphone or as overt as being dared to break rules.

The tricky part? Peer pressure isn't inherently negative. It can push teens to strive for better grades, try out for sports teams, or volunteer in their communities. The key is helping our teens distinguish between positive influences that align with their values and negative pressures that push them away from their authentic selves.

Recognizing unhealthy influences is a crucial skill for teens to develop. Encourage your teen to tune into their inner voice—that gut feeling that something isn't quite right. Are they feeling anxious about fitting in? Do they find themselves acting in ways that don't align with their values? These are red flags that negative peer pressure might be at play.

Here's where the real work begins: equipping your teen with the tools to stand strong in the face of pressure. Assertiveness is like a muscle—it grows stronger with use. Start by role-playing scenarios at home. Practice phrases like, "I appreciate the invite, but I'm not comfortable with that," or "I understand that's your choice, but it's not for me." The goal isn't just to say no, but to do so with confidence and respect.

But standing strong isn't just about what you say—it's about who you surround yourself with. Encourage your teen to seek out friendships that uplift and support them. These are the friends who respect boundaries, celebrate differences, and make your teen feel valued for who they truly are.

Remember, navigating peer pressure is an ongoing process. Encourage your teen to reflect on their experiences through journaling. This practice not only helps process emotions but also serves as a roadmap for future encounters. By understanding their past responses to pressure, they can better prepare for future challenges.

The Importance of Authenticity: Being True to Oneself

Now, let's talk about a concept that's at the heart of resilience and well-being: authenticity. In a world that often seems to demand conformity, being true to oneself is both a challenge and a superpower.

Exploring self-identity is a journey that lasts a lifetime, but it takes center stage during the teenage years. Encourage your teen to dive deep into self-discovery. This might look like keeping a personal journal, trying out different hobbies, or engaging in creative pursuits. The goal is to provide a safe space for your teen to explore who they are, free from judgment or expectation.

But here's the thing about authenticity—it requires courage. Being genuine, especially in group settings, can feel like standing naked in a crowd. It's vulnerable. It's risky. And it's absolutely necessary for building meaningful connections and a strong sense of self.

Talk to your teen about times when they felt pressured to mask their true selves. Maybe it was laughing at a joke they didn't find funny or pretending to like a movie everyone else loved. Now, contrast that with moments when they stood in their truth, even when it wasn't popular. How did each scenario make them feel? Often, we find that while authenticity might be uncomfortable in the moment, it leaves us feeling more aligned and at peace with ourselves in the long run.

Finding the balance between authenticity and conformity is a delicate dance. It's not about being obstinately different or refusing to adapt to social norms. Instead, it's about making conscious choices that honor your true self while still being respectful of others and the situation.

Encourage your teen to think critically about their choices. Are they dressing a certain way because they genuinely like the style, or because they're afraid of standing out? Are they pursuing an activity because it excites them, or because it's what they think they "should" do?

Role-playing can be an incredibly effective tool for practicing authenticity. Set up scenarios where your teen might feel pressured to conform—maybe it's being invited to a party they're not comfortable attending, or being asked their opinion on a controversial topic. Practice responses that are true to their values while still being respectful of others. The goal isn't to create conflict, but to foster the confidence to stand in their truth. Let's try it out.

Exercise: Authenticity Role-Play

Objective

To practice expressing authentic thoughts and feelings in challenging social situations while maintaining respect for others.

Materials

- Index cards
- Pen or pencil
- Timer (optional)

Time: 30-45 minutes

Instructions

1. Scenario Creation (10 minutes):

- Together with your teen, brainstorm 5-6 scenarios where they might feel pressured to conform or hide their true feelings. Write each scenario on an index card.

- Examples: a) Being invited to a party where you know alcohol will be served b) Friends pressuring you to skip class c) Being asked your opinion on a controversial political topic d) Feeling pressured to date someone you're not interested in e) Being encouraged to try a risky activity you're not comfortable with

2. Role-Play Preparation (5 minutes):

- Discuss the importance of balancing authenticity with respect for others.
- Remind your teen that the goal is to express their true feelings and values without creating unnecessary conflict.

3. Role-Play (15-20 minutes):

- Take turns drawing scenario cards.
- The parent plays the role of the person applying pressure, while the teen practices responding authentically.
- Spend about 3-5 minutes on each scenario.
- After each role-play, briefly discuss: • How did it feel to express your authentic thoughts? • What was challenging about the situation? • How did you balance being true to yourself with being respectful?

4. Reflection (5-10 minutes):

- Discuss overall takeaways from the exercise.
- Ask your teen: • Which scenarios felt most challenging? • Did you notice any patterns in how you responded? • How might you apply these skills in real-life situations?

5. Practice Phrases: Encourage your teen to develop a set of go-to phrases that feel authentic to them, such as:

- "I appreciate the invitation, but that's not really my scene."
- "I understand that's your view, but I see it differently."
- "I'm not comfortable with that, but I respect your choice."

Authenticity isn't about being perfect or having it all figured out. It's about being willing to show up as your imperfect, evolving self. Encourage your teen to embrace their quirks, their passions, and yes, even their flaws. These are the things that make them uniquely them.

Making and Keeping Friends: The Value of True Connections

Friendships are the lifeblood of the teenage social world. They provide support, joy, and a sense of belonging. But not all friendships are created equal, and learning to cultivate meaningful connections is a skill that will serve your teen well into adulthood.

Let's start by exploring the qualities of lasting friendships. At their core, strong friendships are built on trust, respect, and mutual understanding. These are relationships where both parties feel seen, heard, and valued. Encourage your teen to reflect on their current friendships. Do they feel they can be themselves around their friends? Do they feel supported in their goals and respected in their choices? These are indicators of healthy, nurturing friendships.

Initiating and nurturing friendships can feel like a daunting task, especially for teens who might be naturally introverted or dealing with social anxiety. The key is to start small and focus on genuine connections rather than popularity. Encourage your teen to strike up conversations based on shared interests. Maybe it's complimenting a classmate's band t-shirt or asking about a book they're reading. These small interactions can be the seeds of deeper connections.

Role-playing can be incredibly helpful here too. Practice conversation starters and active listening skills. Remind your teen that showing genuine interest in others is one of the most attractive qualities a person can have. Encourage them to ask open-ended questions and really listen to the answers.

Of course, even the strongest friendships face challenges. Misunderstandings, jealousy, and conflicting priorities are all normal parts of relationships. The key is how we handle these bumps in the road. Teach your teen to approach conflicts with a mindset of curiosity rather than defensiveness. Instead of jumping to conclusions or assigning blame, encourage them to ask questions and seek to understand the other person's perspective.

Empathy and kindness are the glue that holds friendships together. These qualities create a safe space where both parties feel valued and understood. Encourage your teen to practice small acts of kindness—remembering a friend's important event, offering help without being asked, or simply being there to listen during tough times. These gestures might seem small, but they build a foundation of care and mutual support.

Remember, quality is more important than quantity when it comes to friendships. It's better to have a few deep, meaningful connections than a large circle of superficial acquaintances. Encourage your teen to invest time and energy into the relationships that truly nourish their soul and align with their values.

Dealing with Bullying: Strategies for Teens and Parents

Bullying is a harsh reality that many teens face, and its impact can be devastating. As parents, it's crucial that we equip our teens with the tools to recognize, respond to, and recover from bullying situations. But let's be clear: bullying is not just "kids being kids" or a rite of passage. It's a serious issue that can have long-lasting effects on mental health, self-esteem, and overall well-being.

Recognizing bullying is the first step in addressing it. Bullying can take many forms—physical, verbal, social, or cyber. It's characterized by an imbalance of power, repetition, and intent to harm. Help your teen understand that bullying is never their fault and that they deserve to feel safe and respected.

It's important to note that bullying often happens in subtle ways. Social exclusion, spreading rumors, or even consistent "joking" that makes someone feel uncomfortable can all be forms of bullying. Teach your teen to trust their feelings—if something doesn't feel right, it probably isn't.

Empowering your teen with effective responses to bullying is crucial. This doesn't mean encouraging physical confrontation, but rather teaching assertiveness and self-advocacy. Role-play scenarios where your teen can practice using firm, clear language to stand up to a bully. Phrases like "Stop. I don't like that," or "That's not okay," delivered with confidence, can be powerful.

But let's be real—speaking up can be terrifying, especially when faced with a bully. That's why it's equally important to teach your teen about the power of allies. Encourage them to band together with friends or classmates who share their values. There's strength in numbers, and a united front can often deter bullying behavior.

Equally important is teaching your teen when and how to seek help. Emphasize that reporting bullying is not "tattling"—it's a brave and necessary step to ensure their safety and the safety of others. Help them identify trusted adults they can turn to, whether it's you, a teacher, a school counselor, or a coach.

As parents, our role in addressing bullying is multifaceted. We need to be vigilant for signs that our teen might be experiencing bullying—changes in behavior, reluctance to go to school, or unexplained injuries are all red flags. Create an open, non-judgmental space where your teen feels safe sharing their experiences.

This means being prepared to listen without immediately jumping into "fix-it" mode. Sometimes, our teens just need to be heard and validated. Ask questions like, "How did that make you feel?" and "What do you think you need in this situation?" This approach not only helps your teen process their experiences but also empowers them to be part of the solution.

If your teen is being bullied, take it seriously. Document the incidents, including dates, times, and any witnesses. Don't hesitate to advocate for your teen with school officials. Many schools have anti-bullying policies in place, and it's important that these are enforced. If you feel the school isn't taking appropriate action, don't be afraid to escalate the issue. Your teen's safety and well-being are paramount.

Building a support system is crucial for teens dealing with bullying. This network can include friends, family members, teachers, and mental health professionals if needed. A strong support system provides emotional comfort, practical assistance, and a sense of safety during challenging times.

Consider connecting your teen with a mentor—perhaps an older student or a trusted adult outside the family. Sometimes, teens find it easier to open up to someone who isn't a parent or teacher. This relationship can provide additional support and perspective.

Remember, recovering from bullying takes time. Be patient and continue to provide support even after the immediate situation is resolved. Encourage activities that boost your teen's self-esteem and help them reconnect with their strengths and passions. This might involve sports, arts, volunteering, or any activity where they can experience success and build positive relationships.

It's also important to address the possibility that your teen might be the one engaging in bullying behavior. This can be a difficult reality to face, but it's crucial to address it head-on. If you suspect your teen might be bullying others, approach the situation with empathy and a desire to understand. Often, teens who bully are dealing with their own insecurities or problems. This doesn't excuse the behavior, but understanding the root cause can help in addressing it effectively.

Lastly, let's talk about cyberbullying. In our digital age, bullying doesn't stop when school lets out. It can follow teens home via their devices, making it feel inescapable. Teach your teen about digital citizenship and online safety. This includes how to use privacy settings, the importance of thinking before posting, and how to report abusive behavior on social media platforms.

Encourage your teen to take screenshots of any bullying messages or posts as evidence. Many teens hesitate to report cyberbullying for fear of having their devices taken away. Assure your teen that seeking help won't result in punishment or loss of their digital privileges.

By addressing bullying comprehensively—recognizing it, responding to it, seeking help, and healing from it—we can create a safer, more supportive environment for our teens to thrive in.

Social Media: The Good, The Bad, and The Ugly

In today's digital age, social media is an integral part of most teens' social landscapes. It's a tool that can connect, inspire, and inform—but it also comes with its own set of challenges and pitfalls. As parents, we need to help our teens navigate this digital world with wisdom and intentionality.

Navigating social media wisely starts with understanding its dual nature. On one hand, social media can be a platform for self-expression, creativity, and connection. It can help teens stay in touch with friends, explore interests, and even engage in social activism. Many teens find supportive communities online, particularly those who might feel isolated in their physical communities. For instance, LGBTQ+ teens in conservative areas might find acceptance and resources through online groups.

On the flip side, social media can also be a source of anxiety, comparison, and negativity. The curated nature of social media can create unrealistic expectations about body image, lifestyle, and success. It's crucial to have open conversations with your teen about the reality behind social media posts. Remind them that what they see is often a highlight reel, not the full picture of someone's life.

Discuss with your teen how to use social media intentionally. Encourage them to follow accounts that inspire and uplift them, rather than those that make them feel inadequate or negative about themselves. This might mean unfollowing or muting accounts that consistently make them feel bad about themselves, even if those accounts belong to friends or popular figures.

Talk about the importance of taking breaks from social media and engaging in real-world activities and face-to-face interactions. Many teens (and adults) find it helpful to set specific times for checking social media, rather than constantly scrolling throughout the day. Encourage your teen to try a "digital detox" for a day or a weekend and reflect on how it makes them feel.

Digital footprint awareness is crucial in this age of permanence. Help your teen understand that what they post online can have long-lasting implications. Encourage them to think critically before posting: Is this something they'd be comfortable with a future employer or college admissions officer seeing? Does it align with their values and the image they want to project?

This doesn't mean they can't be themselves online, but rather that they should be mindful of the potential consequences of their digital actions. Teach them about privacy settings and the importance of protecting personal information online.

Dealing with online negativity is unfortunately a common experience for many teens. Teach your teen strategies for handling cyberbullying, negative comments, and the pressure of comparison that often comes with social media use. This might include using blocking and reporting features, setting boundaries around social media use, and knowing when to step away from the digital world to protect their mental health.

Encourage your teen to be a positive force in their online communities. This could mean standing up against cyberbullying when they see it, sharing uplifting content, or using their platform to support causes they care about. Remind them that their online actions can have a real impact on others, for better or worse.

Discuss the concept of digital empathy—the ability to understand and share the feelings of others in online interactions. Encourage your teen to consider how their words might be interpreted without the context of tone and body language. Teach them to err on the side of kindness in their online communications.

It's also important to address the addictive nature of social media. Many platforms are designed to keep users engaged for as long as possible, which can interfere with sleep, homework, and real-life social interactions. Help your teen recognize signs that their social media use might be problematic, such as feeling anxious when they can't check their phone or losing track of time while scrolling.

Lastly, model healthy social media habits yourself. Be mindful of your own digital consumption and how you present yourself online. Your example can be a powerful influence on your teen's relationship with social media. This might mean putting your phone away during family dinners, avoiding mindless scrolling, and sharing your own reflections on how social media impacts your mood and behavior.

Remember, the goal isn't to demonize social media—it's a powerful tool that's here to stay. Instead, we want to empower our teens to use it wisely and intentionally, leveraging its benefits while mitigating its potential harms. By fostering open dialogue and critical thinking about social media, we can help our teens develop a healthy, balanced approach to their digital lives.

Exercise: Social Scenario Role-Play Workshop

Now, let's put all of this into practice with an interactive workshop designed to help your teen navigate various social scenarios with confidence and authenticity.

Objective

To practice navigating various social situations through role-play, enhancing communication skills and confidence.

Materials

- Index cards with different social scenarios
- Timer
- Notepad for feedback

Instructions

1. Together with your teen, brainstorm various social scenarios they might encounter. These could include dealing with peer pressure, resolving a misunderstanding with a friend, standing up to a bully, or navigating a difficult conversation on social media. Write each scenario on an index card.

2. Take turns drawing a card and acting out the scenario. The teen plays themselves, while the adult plays the other character(s). This gives your teen a chance to practice their responses in a safe, supportive environment.

3. After each 5-minute role-play, spend 5 minutes discussing:

- What went well?
- What could be improved?
- How did it feel to handle the situation?

4. Switch roles occasionally, allowing the teen to play different characters and the adult to model effective responses. This can provide your teen with new perspectives and strategies they might not have considered.

5. Conclude the session by discussing overall learnings and strategies that seemed most effective across different scenarios. What patterns emerged? What skills does your teen feel most confident about, and where do they feel they need more practice?

This activity provides a safe space for teens to practice social skills and receive constructive feedback, building their confidence for real-world interactions. It's also an opportunity for you to gain insight into the challenges your teen faces and how they approach problem-solving in social situations.

Navigating the social landscape of adolescence is no small feat. It requires courage, self-awareness, and a willingness to stand in one's truth even when it's uncomfortable. By guiding your teen through these aspects of social navigation—understanding peer pressure, embracing authenticity, cultivating meaningful friendships, addressing bullying, and navigating the digital world—you're equipping them with invaluable tools for not just surviving, but thriving in their social world.

Your role is to provide support, guidance, and a safe harbor as they learn to navigate these complex social waters. You're not just helping them develop social skills; you're nurturing their ability to form deep, meaningful connections while staying true to themselves. And in doing so, you're setting them up for a lifetime of rich, authentic relationships and a strong sense of self.

SEVEN

Activities for Building Social Skills

I n a period where the digital world frequently overshadows the physical, finding balance can feel like steering a boat through fog —challenging yet essential for reaching our destination safely. This chapter focuses on practical exercises that foster genuine connections, aiming to ground us in the tangible aspects of human interaction. These exercises are designed not just to draw us away from screens, but to bring us closer to one another, strengthening bonds through shared experiences that go beyond digital likes and comments.

As we begin this chapter, it's important to address a common concern: how do we convince teenagers to willingly participate in these family activities? Parents might already be anticipating resistance, while teens might be thinking these exercises sound unappealing or unnecessary.

The teenage years are typically a time of seeking independence, testing boundaries, and often, a desire to distance oneself from family activities. The suggestions in this book might initially seem unattractive to a teen. However, with the right approach, even skeptical teens can find value and enjoyment in these exercises.

Understanding the Teen Perspective

It's crucial to recognize where teens are coming from. They're navigating a complex world of social pressures, academic stress, and personal identity formation. Their resistance often isn't about rejecting family, but about asserting their growing independence and individuality.

Strategies for Engagement

1. **Involve Them in the Planning**: Instead of presenting activities as mandatory, include your teen in the decision-making process. Ask for their input on which activities interest them or how they might modify an exercise to make it more appealing.
2. **Explain the 'Why'**: Teens are more likely to participate if they understand the purpose. Have an open conversation about the goals of these activities – strengthening family bonds, reducing stress, improving communication – and how these skills can benefit them in their own lives.
3. **Start Small and Build**: Don't expect immediate enthusiasm for a full day of family activities. Begin with shorter, less intrusive exercises and gradually increase the time and complexity as comfort and interest grow.
4. **Make it Relevant**: Connect the activities to things your teen cares about. For example, if they're into sports, relate mindfulness exercises to improving athletic performance.
5. **Lead by Example**: Show your own willingness to try new things. Share your experiences and the benefits you've noticed from these activities.
6. **Respect Their Space**: Recognize that teens need their alone time. Balance family activities with respect for their privacy and independence.

7. **Use Technology Positively**: Instead of framing these activities as anti-technology, find ways to incorporate tech positively. You might use a meditation app together or create a family playlist for background music during activities.
8. **Be Patient and Persistent**: Change takes time. Stay positive and keep offering opportunities for engagement without forcing participation.

The goal isn't to force teens into unwanted activities but to create an environment where they feel respected, heard, and genuinely interested in participating. With patience, understanding, and the right approach, even reluctant teens can come to appreciate and look forward to these family bonding experiences.

In the following sections, we'll explore specific activities designed to navigate the challenges of our digital age and reconnect with the physical world. We'll discuss how to tailor them to appeal to the teenage mindset, ensuring that your whole family, including your teens, can benefit from these exercises in connection and mindfulness. Our aim is to create a balanced approach that acknowledges the realities of our digital age while fostering the irreplaceable value of face-to-face human connections.

Digital Detox Challenges: Promoting Offline Interaction

Imagine: it's Sunday morning, and instead of the usual symphony of notification pings and the glow of screens illuminating sleepy faces, there's... silence. Actual, honest-to-goodness silence. Welcome to the Digital Detox!

Without the constant digital noise, we suddenly have space. Space to talk, to laugh, to be bored together. We rediscover the art of eye contact and the joy of finishing a sentence without checking a notification.

This isn't about demonizing technology. It's about remembering that there's a whole world of joy and connection beyond our screens.

Exercise: Plan a Digital Detox Day

Now, let's put this into practice with an interactive workshop designed to help your family disconnect from digital devices and reconnect with each other.

Objective

To experience a full day without digital devices, promoting unfiltered, continuous real-world interactions and strengthening family bonds.

Materials

- Calendar for planning
- List of offline activities
- Box or container for storing devices
- Journals or notepads for reflection

Instructions

1. As a family, choose a day of the week to designate as your "digital detox day." Mark it on the calendar.

2. Create a list of offline activities that don't require digital devices. Include options for various interests and weather conditions.

3. On the chosen day, have each family member turn off their cell phones, tablets, and computers. Store them in a designated container.

4. Engage in the planned offline activities throughout the day. Encourage face-to-face conversations and collaborative activities.

5. At the end of the day, hold a family meeting to reflect on the experience. Discuss:

- What did each person enjoy most about the day?
- What challenges did they face?
- What did they learn about themselves and each other?

6. Plan how to incorporate more offline time into your regular daily life.

7. Schedule the next digital detox day, making it a recurring family event.

This activity creates a space where everyone can be fully present, engaging in conversation and reconnecting on a deeper level. It strengthens family bonds and fosters a healthier relationship with technology, reminding everyone of the joy that exists beyond the digital realm. However, it's important to recognize that this might be challenging at first, especially for those accustomed to constant digital connectivity. If that's the case, start small and gradually work your way up to a full day. Begin with a few hours of device-free time, then try a half-day, slowly increasing the duration as everyone becomes more comfortable with the practice. This gradual approach allows family members to adjust and discover the benefits at their own pace.

Exercise: Creative Projects Without Screens

Imagine your family huddled around a giant canvas, paintbrushes flying. You're not just making art; you're building memories, sharing laughs, and having those rare, uninterrupted conversations. Maybe you'll write a story together, each adding your own twists. Suddenly, your 8-year-old's obsession with dinosaurs, your teenager's love for sci-fi, and your partner's terrible puns all come together in one hilariously bizarre tale.

These aren't just fun activities – they're stealth exercises for family bonding and brain power. You're nurturing creativity, critical thinking, and communication skills, all while creating inside jokes that'll last for years.

Let's explore how creativity can flourish in the absence of digital distractions.

Objective

To engage in creative activities that promote self-expression, family bonding, and mental stimulation without the use of digital devices.

Materials

- Art supplies (e.g., paints, brushes, paper, clay)
- Musical instruments (if available)
- Writing materials
- Any other craft supplies relevant to your chosen project

Instructions

1. As a family, brainstorm creative projects you'd like to try. Options might include:

- Painting or drawing
- Making music
- Writing stories or poems
- Crafting (e.g., knitting, woodworking, scrapbooking)

2. Choose one or more projects that interest everyone.

3. Gather the necessary supplies for your chosen project(s).

4. Set aside dedicated time for the family to work on the project(s) together.

5. As you create, encourage discussion about thoughts, feelings, and ideas inspired by the creative process.

6. Once the project(s) are complete, have each family member share their creation and what it means to them.

7. Reflect on the experience:

- How did it feel to create without digital assistance?
- What new things did you learn about yourself or your family members?
- How did this activity contribute to family bonding?

These exercises empower creative expression while also enhancing cognitive skills such as problem-solving and critical thinking. They develop familial ties through shared creative endeavors, celebrating both individuality and solidarity.

Exercise: Outdoor Adventure Challenge

Want to see your kids' eyes light up with something other than screen glow? It's time to head outdoors!

Swapping Netflix for nature isn't just about escaping Wi-Fi range; it's about plugging into a whole new (or rather, very old) way of living. Whether you're hiking, biking, or just having a chaotic family game of tag, you're not just burning calories—you're building connections.

Picture this: Your family is tackling a local trail. Suddenly, your couch potato teen is leading the way, your usually shy 8-year-old is shouting encouragement, and you're all working together to decipher that suspiciously coffee-stained map. It's like a real-life video game, but with fresh air and no respawn button.

These adventures aren't just fun – they're secret weapons for family bonding. You're problem-solving, communicating, and high-fiving your way up that hill. Plus, you're all getting a healthy dose of vitamin D and exercise without a single complaint about "boring" workouts.

Best of all? You're showing your kids that the world is bigger than their screens. Now, let's venture outside and experience the freedom and connection that nature offers.

Objective

To engage in outdoor activities that promote physical health, family cooperation, and appreciation for the natural world.

Materials

- Appropriate outdoor gear (depending on the chosen activity)
- Water and snacks
- First aid kit
- Map or trail guide (if necessary)

Instructions

1. As a family, choose an outdoor activity suitable for everyone's abilities. Options might include:

- Hiking a local trail
- Biking in a park
- Playing a team sport in the backyard
- Going on a nature scavenger hunt

2. Plan the details of your adventure, including location, duration, and any necessary preparations.

3. Assign roles to family members (e.g., navigator, photographer, snack coordinator).

4. During the activity, encourage cooperation and communication. For example:

- Navigate the trail together
- Cheer each other on during challenging parts
- Point out interesting natural features to one another

5. Take breaks to appreciate your surroundings and discuss what you're experiencing.

6. After the adventure, gather as a family to reflect:

- What was the most enjoyable part of the experience?
- What challenges did you overcome together?
- What did you learn about nature or each other?

7. Discuss how you can incorporate more outdoor activities into your regular routine.

These experiences are not only physically beneficial but also mentally and emotionally enriching. They provide fresh air, exercise, and the joy of achieving a goal together, while fostering an appreciation for nature and the environment.

Exercise: Digital Detox Reflection Workshop

Digital detox complete, now for the fun part—the family debrief.

Huddle up and reflect. What worked well? What was tough? What surprises popped up when the screens went dark? This chat isn't just for warm fuzzies – it's cementing those screen-free lessons and plotting how to integrate more unplugged moments into daily life.

One day of digital detox is great, but a life peppered with screen-free adventures? That's the golden ticket. These little pockets of unplugged time are like seasoning in life's sometimes-bland casserole, reminding us that the world is a 3D experience no screen can match.

To conclude our digital detox challenges, let's reflect on our experiences and plan for the future.

Objective

To consolidate learnings from the digital detox experiences and integrate offline activities into daily life.

Materials

- Journals or notepads
- Pens or pencils
- Whiteboard or large paper for group brainstorming
- Calendar for future planning

Instructions

1. Gather as a family in a comfortable space.

2. Each family member should take a few minutes to write down their thoughts about the digital detox experiences, including:

- What they enjoyed most
- What they found challenging
- What they learned about themselves and others

3. Take turns sharing these reflections with the family.

4. As a group, discuss:

- How did the absence of digital devices affect family interactions?
- What unexpected benefits or challenges did you encounter?
- How did these experiences change your perspective on technology use?

5. Brainstorm ways to integrate more offline activities into your daily life. Write these ideas on the whiteboard or large paper.

6. Create a family action plan:

- Choose 2-3 offline activities to incorporate into your weekly routine
- Decide on the frequency of future digital detox days
- Assign responsibilities for planning and organizing these activities

7. Mark these plans on your family calendar.

8. Commit to reviewing and adjusting your plan monthly to ensure it continues to meet your family's needs.

This reflection process solidifies the lessons learned from these experiences, reinforcing the benefits of time spent offline. It provides a platform for discussing how to integrate more of these activities into regular daily life, ensuring that the digital detox isn't just a one-off event but part of a broader commitment to nurturing real connections and well-being.

Emotional Intelligence Games: Learning Through Play

Integrating Emotional Intelligence (EI) games into your family's routine offers a wonderful method for enhancing your child's comprehension and management of emotions while fostering deeper family connections. These games, ranging from board games to role-playing situations, provide both fun and educational experiences that help develop essential emotional abilities such as empathy, acknowledgment, and guidance.

Exercise: Empathy Board Game Night

Ever wish you could download empathy directly into your teen's brain? Well, we can't do that (yet), but we've got the next best thing: Empathy Board Game Night! It's time to dust off those board games and turn them into secret weapons of emotional intelligence. Imagine a family game night where the real prize isn't just winning, but understanding each other better. We're talking about games that'll have your teen considering others' feelings faster than they can say "You sank my battleship!" So, grab your dice, settle in, and get ready for a night of fun that sneakily builds emotional skills. Who knew Boardwalk could be a pathway to better relationships?

Objective

To develop empathy and emotional understanding through interactive board games.

Materials

- Empathy-focused board games (e.g., 'Empathy Is Your Superpower', 'The Compassion Game')
- Comfortable seating arrangement
- Snacks (optional, but recommended for a cozy atmosphere)

Instructions

1. Choose an empathy-focused board game suitable for your family's age range.

2. Set up the game in a comfortable area where everyone can gather around easily.

3. Before starting, explain that the goal is not just to win, but to understand and relate to the emotions presented in the game.

4. As you play, encourage discussions about the emotions and situations presented in the game. Ask questions like:

- "How do you think this character feels?"
- "What would you do in this situation?"
- "Have you ever felt similar to this?"

5. After each round or significant moment in the game, take a brief pause to reflect on the emotional aspects of what just happened.

6. At the end of the game, have a family discussion:

- What new things did you learn about emotions?
- Did anyone surprise you with their insights?
- How can you apply what you learned to real-life situations?

7. Plan your next empathy game night, perhaps rotating game choices or allowing different family members to lead.

This exercise improves your teen's ability to relate well and opens up family conversations about feelings, making it easier to discuss sentiments and real-life circumstances.

Exercise: Emotional Journey Video Game Session

Imagine using that game console for something other than virtual car theft or building block worlds. Welcome to the Emotional Journey Video Game Session, where button-mashing meets heart-string-tugging. We're talking about games that'll have your teen feeling all the feels—and then talking about them! It's like sneaking vegetables into a smoothie, but instead, we're blending emotional intelligence into gameplay. So, grab a controller, settle into the couch, and get ready to navigate digital worlds and real emotions together. Who knows? You might just level up your family's emotional intelligence while saving a virtual world or two.

Objective

To use video games as a tool for exploring emotional situations and decision-making.

Materials

- A video game console or computer
- Selected video games with emotional storylines (e.g., 'Journey', 'Rime')
- Comfortable seating for the family

Instructions

1. Choose a video game known for its emotional storytelling or themes.

2. Before starting, explain that you'll be playing together to explore the emotional journey of the characters.

3. Take turns playing, or have one person play while others observe.

4. Pause the game at key emotional moments to discuss:

- What emotions is the character experiencing?
- What led to this emotional state?
- How is the character dealing with these emotions?
- What would you do in this situation?

5. After playing for a set time (e.g., 1 hour), have a family discussion:

- What was the most impactful emotional moment in the game?
- Did any character's emotional journey resonate with you personally?
- What strategies for handling emotions did you observe in the game?
- How can these insights apply to real-life situations?

6. Consider creating a family "emotional strategy guide" based on what you learned from the game.

By examining the emotional journeys within these games, you can assist your teen in pondering their own feelings and learn valuable lessons about emotional resilience and empathy.

Communication Role-Play: Practicing Real-Life Scenarios

We're about to turn your living room into a bootcamp for budding conversationalists. Forget reading about communication skills—that's like trying to learn parkour from a PowerPoint presentation. Your teen needs to dive into the verbal obstacle course of real life, and role-playing is their safety harness. It's time to create a judgment-free zone where they can practice everything from negotiating curfew extensions to explaining suspicious dents in the car, all without the risk of actual grounding. Think of it as a live-action video game where leveling up means fewer foot-in-mouth moments and more "How did my kid get so articulate?" moments. So, grab your imaginary microphones and let the awkward begin—because in this game, embracing the cringe is how you win.

Exercise: Difficult Conversations Simulator

Ever wish you could practice those cringe-worthy talks before they happen in real life? Well, now you can! Think of it as a flight simulator, but instead of learning to land a plane, you're learning to land points in a debate about curfew extension. We're creating a judgment-free zone where your teen can practice everything from confronting a gossipy friend to explaining a bad grade, all without the risk of actual consequence. It's like a real-life video game where the boss level is "Explaining to Dad why there's a dent in the car" without losing screen time privileges.

Objective

To practice navigating challenging conversations and conflicts in a supportive environment.

Materials

- Index cards with various difficult conversation scenarios
- Timer
- Optional: props to set the scene

Instructions

1. As a family, brainstorm potential difficult conversations teens might face (e.g., confronting a friend about a betrayal, discussing a bad grade with a teacher).

2. Write each scenario on an index card.

3. Set up a "stage" area in your living room.

4. Take turns drawing a card and acting out the scenario. One person plays the teen, another plays the other party, and the rest of the family observes.

5. Act out the conversation for 5 minutes.

6. After each scenario, have a 5-minute family discussion:

- What strategies worked well?
- What could have been handled differently?
- How did it feel to be in each role?

7. Switch roles and try the scenario again, incorporating the feedback.

8. At the end of the session, reflect on:

- Common effective strategies across different scenarios
- Personal strengths and areas for improvement in communication
- How to apply these skills in real-life situations

This exercise helps teens develop a toolbox of responses, from de-escalating tension to asserting their viewpoint in a respectful way. It encourages them to consider the impact of their words and actions, fostering a deeper understanding of how to maintain relationships even through conflicts.

Exercise: Assertiveness Training Camp

It's time to help your teen find their voice without turning into a mini Gordon Ramsay. Think of it as charm school, but instead of teaching which fork to use, we're teaching how to use words to stand up for themselves. We'll practice scenarios ranging from "No, I don't want to try that suspicious-looking substance" to "Actually, I disagree with that opinion." It's all about finding that sweet spot between doormat and jerk. So, lace up those metaphorical boots, and let's start training those assertiveness muscles.

Objective

To practice assertive communication in various scenarios.

Materials

- List of scenarios requiring assertiveness (e.g., setting boundaries, refusing peer pressure)
- "I statement" formula sheet: "I feel [emotion] when [situation] because [reason]. I would like [request]."
- Optional: video recording device for playback and analysis

Instructions

1. Introduce the concept of assertiveness and its importance.

2. Review the "I statement" formula and practice creating a few as a family.

3. Present a scenario (e.g., "Your friend wants to copy your homework").

4. Have your teen respond assertively using the "I statement" formula.

5. Family members provide constructive feedback:

- Was the message clear?
- How was the tone and body language?
- Did it strike a balance between assertive and respectful?

6. If using a camera, review the recording together for additional insights.

7. Practice the scenario again, incorporating the feedback.

8. Repeat with different scenarios, rotating roles among family members.

9. Conclude with a reflection:

- Which scenarios were most challenging?
- How did it feel to communicate assertively?
- How can these skills be applied in daily life?

This training improves teens' interpersonal skills and boosts their confidence as they learn to stand up for themselves in various situations.

Exercise: Interview Simulation Studio

Welcome to the Interview Simulation Studio, where we turn those nerve-wracking job interviews into Oscar-worthy performances. It's time to prepare your teen for the real world, one awkward handshake at a time. We're talking mock interviews that'll make your palms sweat but in a good way. From "Tell me about yourself" to "Where do you see yourself in five years?" (spoiler alert: not in this interview), we'll cover it all. We'll work on everything from firm handshakes to eye contact that says "hire me" instead of "help me."

Objective

To prepare teens for various interview situations through practice and feedback.

Materials

- List of common interview questions
- Professional attire (optional, but can help set the mood)
- Video recording device (if possible)
- "Interview Feedback" sheets

Instructions

1. Set up a mock interview space (e.g., a desk and two chairs).

2. Choose an interview scenario (job application, college admission, etc.).

3. Assign roles: interviewer, interviewee, and observers.

4. Conduct a 10-15 minute mock interview.

5. Observers take notes on:

- Verbal responses
- Non-verbal cues (eye contact, posture, gestures)
- Overall presentation

6. After the interview, provide constructive feedback:

- Interviewee shares how they felt
- Interviewer gives their impressions
- Observers share their notes

7. If recorded, watch the video together and discuss additional observations.

8. Practice specific elements that need improvement (e.g., answering a tricky question, maintaining eye contact).

9. Switch roles and repeat the process.

10. Conclude with a family discussion:

- What were the biggest learnings?
- How can these skills be applied to other life situations?
- Plan for ongoing interview practice sessions

This thorough approach ensures that teens not only learn how to express their thoughts clearly but also how to present themselves professionally, expanding their confidence and poise in real interview situations.

Building a Support Network: Encouraging Peer Support

Navigating the teenage years can be like sailing through uncharted waters, where each social interaction can potentially either storm or sparkle. During this stage, the importance of a strong support network couldn't be greater. It provides a safety net to catch a teen when they falter, as well as a cheering squad to celebrate their triumphs.

Exercise: Peer Support Group Starter Kit

It's time to help your kids find their tribe with our Peer Support Group Starter Kit. Think of it as building a real-life social network, minus the trolls and cat videos. We're creating a space where teens can share their dramas, traumas, and occasional "eureka!" moments with peers who get it. It's like a support group meets a cool hangout spot, where the only thing being shared is understanding (and maybe some snacks). Whether your teen is stressed about school, navigating the social jungle, or just trying to figure out why their left eyebrow won't cooperate, this group is their safe haven.

Objective

To establish or join a peer support group that provides a safe space for teens to share experiences and solutions.

Materials

- List of potential peer support group themes
- Guidelines for respectful communication
- Notebook for planning meetings
- Snacks (because teens + food = success)

Instructions

1. Discuss with your teen the concept of a peer support group and its benefits.

2. Brainstorm potential themes for the group (e.g., academic stress, social dynamics, personal growth).

3. Decide whether to join an existing group or start a new one:

- If joining: Research local groups and attend a meeting together
- If starting: Move to step 4

4. For a new group:

- Help your teen invite peers who might be interested
- Choose a regular meeting time and place
- Establish group guidelines for respect and confidentiality

5. Plan the first meeting:

- Create an icebreaker activity
- Prepare a topic for discussion
- Set up the meeting space to be welcoming and comfortable

6. After the first meeting, reflect with your teen:

- What went well?
- What could be improved?
- How did it feel to share and listen to peers?

7. Encourage regular attendance and possibly rotating leadership roles.

8. Check in periodically about the group's impact and any support needed.

The beauty of these groups lies in their foundation of mutual respect and empathy, which can significantly enhance each member's ability to cope with stress and build resilience.

Exercise: Mentorship Match-Up

We're on a mission to connect your budding teenager with a wise sage who's been there, done that, and got the t-shirt (probably with an inspirational quote on it). This isn't about finding someone to nag them about homework; it's about discovering a guide who can show them the ropes of life, career, or maybe just how to adult without burning down the kitchen. Whether your teen is a budding artist, a future CEO, or just trying to figure out their path, we'll help them find a mentor who can light the way.

Objective

To connect teens with mentors who can provide guidance, encouragement, and support.

Materials

- List of your teen's interests and goals
- Directory of local mentorship programs
- Notebook for mentor meeting notes

Instructions

1. Sit down with your teen and discuss the concept of mentorship:

- What is a mentor?
- How can a mentor be helpful?
- What qualities would they want in a mentor?

2. Make a list of your teen's interests, goals, and areas where they'd like guidance.

3. Research mentorship opportunities:

- School programs
- Community organizations
- Professional associations in areas of interest

4. Help your teen reach out to potential mentors or mentorship programs.

5. Prepare for the first mentor meeting:

- Brainstorm questions to ask
- Set some initial goals for the mentorship

6. After the first meeting, reflect with your teen:

- How did it go?
- Do they feel this mentor is a good fit?
- What do they hope to gain from the relationship?

7. Encourage regular check-ins about the mentorship:

- What are they learning?
- How is it helping them grow?
- Are there any challenges?

8. If your teen shows leadership potential, discuss the possibility of them becoming a mentor to younger peers.

Mentors can help teens set realistic goals, encourage them to step out of their comfort zones, and provide a safe space to discuss fears and disappointments without judgment.

Exercise: Community Service Adventure

Welcome to the Community Service Adventure, where we're saving the world one good deed at a time. It's like a family vacation, but instead of getting sunburned and arguing over maps, you're making a difference and feeling warm fuzzies. We're talking about activities that'll have your teen realizing that "influencer" can mean more than just having a million followers. From serving meals at a soup kitchen to planting trees or teaching grandma how to video call, we're about to embark on a journey that's part charity, part family bonding, and all heart.

Objective

To engage in community service activities that build connections, instill a sense of purpose, and develop social empathy.

Materials

- List of local volunteer opportunities
- Calendar for planning
- Any necessary supplies for the chosen activity

Instructions

1. As a family, research local community service opportunities:

- Local clean-up events
- Food banks
- Animal shelters
- Senior centers or healthcare centers
- Environmental conservation projects

2. Discuss which causes resonate most with your family values.

3. Choose a community service activity that everyone can participate in.

4. Prepare for the activity:

- Sign up or register if necessary
- Gather any required supplies
- Discuss expectations and goals

5. Participate in the chosen community service activity together.

6. After the activity, have a family reflection session:

- What did each person enjoy most?
- What was challenging?
- What did you learn about the community or each other?
- How did it feel to make a difference?

7. Discuss how to make community service a regular part of your family routine.

8. Plan your next service activity, perhaps trying something new or building on this experience.

These activities can significantly widen a teen's circle of connections and develop their understanding of teamwork and community engagement. Moreover, working toward a shared goal can create a sense of camaraderie and accomplishment among participants, strengthening the bonds between them.

Family Activities: Strengthening Bonds and Skills Together

Family time is more than just an opportunity to be together; it's a chance to weave stronger social threads that not only connect but also fortify each family member against life's inevitable challenges. Organizing activities that involve all family members can transform everyday moments into memories and lessons that last a lifetime.

Exercise: Family Game Night Championship

Forget about mind-numbing screen time; we're talking old-school, face-to-face fun that'll have everyone forgetting to check their phones. From classic board games to charades that'll leave you in stitches, we're creating a weekly tradition that's part bonding, part brain-teasing, and all awesome. It's a chance for your teen to showcase their strategic brilliance, for Dad to finally use that obscure trivia knowledge, and for Mom to reveal her hidden talent for miming "underwater basket weaving." Let's turn game night into the highlight of the week!

Objective

To foster communication, cooperation, and healthy competition through regular family game nights.

Materials

- A variety of board games, card games, or interactive games
- Scoreboard or trophy (optional, for added excitement)
- Snacks and beverages
- Calendar for scheduling

Instructions

1. As a family, choose a regular night for your game championship (e.g., every Friday).

2. Create a roster of games that appeal to different family members, including:

- Strategy games
- Cooperative games
- Quick, fun games
- Educational games

3. Establish some ground rules for fair play and good sportsmanship.

4. On game night:

- Take turns choosing the game
- Mix up teams or partnerships if applicable
- Encourage discussion and laughter throughout

5. After each game, have a quick debrief:

- What strategies worked well?
- How did teamwork play a role?
- What was the most enjoyable part?

6. Keep a running scoreboard or pass a trophy to create a sense of ongoing championship (if desired).

7. At the end of each month, reflect as a family:

- What were the favorite games?
- How has game night affected the family dynamic?
- Any new games to add to the rotation?

These game nights' laughter and camaraderie can significantly strengthen familial bonds, making them cherished traditions that reinforce the family as a unit.

Exercise: Master Chef Family Edition

Attention all kitchen novices and culinary maestros! It's time to turn dinner prep into a delicious adventure with Master Chef Family Edition. We're not just cooking meals; we're serving up a big plate of family bonding with a side of life skills. Picture this: your teen chopping veggies (with all fingers intact), your partner mastering the art of not burning water, and you orchestrating it all like a seasoned conductor. It's part cooking show, part comedy routine, and all delicious. We'll tackle family recipes, explore new cuisines, and maybe even invent a dish or two (Spaghetti Tacos, anyone?). Along the way, we'll stir in some teamwork, sprinkle in some problem-solving, and garnish it all with hearty laughs. Let's turn dinner prep into a delicious adventure!

Objective

To transform meal preparation into a collaborative family activity that teaches life skills, encourages teamwork, and creates opportunities for meaningful conversations.

Materials

- Recipes (family favorites or new challenges)
- Cooking utensils and ingredients
- Aprons for everyone (optional, but fun!)
- Music playlist for cooking ambiance

Instructions

1. Choose a regular day for family cooking (e.g., Sunday dinners).

2. As a family, plan the menu:

- Rotate who gets to choose the main dish
- Ensure everyone has a role in the meal preparation

3. Assign roles based on age and ability:

- Younger kids can measure or mix
- Teens can take on more complex tasks
- Adults can supervise and handle any dangerous tasks

4. Before cooking, have a quick "team meeting":

- Review the recipe and game plan
- Discuss any potential challenges
- Assign a timekeeper to keep things on schedule

5. Cook together, encouraging conversation throughout:

- Share family stories or traditions related to the dish
- Discuss everyone's day or upcoming events
- Ask open-ended questions to spark deeper discussions

6. Set the table together and enjoy the meal as a family.

7. During the meal, reflect on the cooking process:

- What was the most enjoyable part?
- What new skills did everyone learn?
- How did teamwork contribute to the final result?

8. Plan the next family cooking session, perhaps with a new cuisine or cooking challenge.

This activity not only teaches valuable life skills like cooking but also fosters coordination and communication in a relaxed setting. The conversations that flow while chopping vegetables or stirring a pot often delve into topics that might not arise in more formal settings, creating a casual atmosphere where family members are comfortable opening up about various subjects.

Exercise: Cultural Exploration Expedition

Pack your imaginary bags and grab your metaphorical passports – it's time for a Cultural Exploration Expedition, right from your living room! We're turning your home into a launchpad for worldwide adventures, no jet lag required. Each month, we'll "visit" a new country or culture, immersing ourselves in everything from its cuisine to its customs. It's like a crash course in global citizenship, but with comfier seating. We'll learn to say "hello" in new languages, attempt to recreate iconic dishes (with varying degrees of success), and maybe even try on traditional outfits (embarrassing family photos, anyone?). It's a chance to broaden horizons, challenge stereotypes, and maybe discover that your teen has a hidden talent for Bollywood dancing or origami. So, spin that globe, pick a destination, and let's embark on a journey that'll make your family the most cultured on the block.

Objective

To broaden family perspectives and foster curiosity about different cultures through planned cultural exploration activities.

Materials

- World map or globe
- Cultural exploration resources (books, documentaries, websites)
- Materials for related crafts or activities
- Ingredients for cooking cultural dishes (if applicable)

Instructions

1. As a family, choose a culture or country to explore each month.

2. Create a "Cultural Exploration Checklist" for each expedition:

- Learn basic phrases in the language
- Cook a traditional meal
- Watch a film or documentary about the culture
- Create art inspired by the culture
- Listen to traditional music
- Read a book by an author from that culture

3. Designate roles for each family member in the exploration:

- Cultural Cuisine Chef
- Language Learner
- Art Director

- History Buff
- Music Maestro

4. Throughout the month, engage in activities from your checklist.

5. Have a "Cultural Celebration Night" at the end of the month:

- Prepare and enjoy a meal from the culture
- Share what each person learned in their role
- Discuss similarities and differences with your own culture
- Reflect on how this exploration changed your perspectives

6. Choose the next culture to explore, perhaps letting a different family member pick each time.

These cultural exploration activities can significantly expand your family's perspectives, fostering a sense of curiosity and openness. They provide a context for discussing different viewpoints and narratives, enhancing your teens' understanding of the world. Such experiences can spark interest in areas your teen may not have encountered otherwise, potentially leading to new hobbies or academic interests.

As we wrap up this chapter, let's take a moment to appreciate the power of these family activities. They're more than just ways to pass the time; they're opportunities to strengthen your family bonds and help your teens develop crucial life skills.

Each exercise, from game nights to volunteer projects, serves a dual purpose. They're fun in the moment, sure, but they're also building blocks for your teen's future. We're talking about developing empathy, honing communication skills, and fostering a sense of community responsibility - all disguised as family time.

These shared experiences create a tapestry of memories and learning moments. They transform ordinary days into opportunities for growth, extending your family's connections both with each other and the wider world. They help cultivate compassion, teamwork, and social awareness in ways that lectures or rules simply can't match.

As you move forward, remember that these activities aren't just about today. They're shaping your family's story and equipping your teens with valuable skills and perspectives they'll carry into adulthood. The conversations you have, the challenges you overcome together, and the memories you create - these are the threads that will continue to connect your family, even as your teens grow and change.

So, keep at it, parents. These shared moments aren't just shaping your days; they're molding your family's future, creating bonds and developing abilities that will resonate far beyond the time spent together. Your investment in these activities is an investment in your family's long-term happiness and your teen's future success.

EIGHT

Supporting Your Teen's Journey

Navigating the teenage years can often feel like deciphering a complex map without a legend, especially when it comes to communication. Every interaction, every silence, holds a nuance that can seem puzzling at first. However, as you embark on guiding your teenager through these formative years, the power of open and effective communication cannot be overstated. It forms the foundation upon which trust is built and understanding grows, enabling your teen to confidently explore their social, emotional, and academic landscapes.

Starting the Conversation: Tips for Open Dialogue

Creating a safe space for dialogue is crucial. Teens need to feel that their thoughts and feelings are respected and valued. This goes beyond just providing a quiet, comfortable physical setting; it's about cultivating an emotional atmosphere where they feel secure. Start by affirming your teen's perspective, showing appreciation for their openness, and validating their feelings, even when you don't fully understand or agree with them. This doesn't mean refraining from guidance or feedback, but rather ensuring that your initial response is one of acceptance. Such an environment encourages your teen to share more freely and honestly, reducing the fear of judgment or dismissal.

Active listening is a skill that requires practice and patience, especially with teenagers whose communication styles can be as varied as their moods. To master this art, focus on truly hearing what your teen is saying without planning your response or judgment. This involves giving them your full attention—putting aside devices, making eye contact, nodding, or making small verbal acknowledgments to show you're engaged. Consider what you've heard by summarizing their points, asking clarifying questions, and expressing empathy. For instance, if your teen is upset about falling out with a friend, you might say, "It sounds like you're really hurt because you feel betrayed. Is that right?" Such responses demonstrate that you're listening and connecting with their emotional experience.

Keeping the conversation flowing often relies on how questions are framed. Open-ended questions, as opposed to those with yes or no answers, encourage deeper reflection and more elaborate responses, paving the way for richer dialogue. Instead of asking, "Did you have a good day at school?" try, "What was the most interesting thing you learned today?" or "How did the group project discussion go?" These questions invite your teen to share their thoughts and feelings in more depth, providing insights into their world and helping you understand their perspectives better.

Regular check-ins are vital for maintaining open lines of communication. Sometimes, the rhythm of our daily lives can sweep us along, making it easy to let communication with our teen become transactional—about schedules, chores, and responsibilities. Instituting regular, casual check-ins can break this pattern, ensuring ongoing open dialogue. These check-ins can be as simple as a chat over a snack after school or a walk after dinner. Consistency and a non-pressuring atmosphere are key. These moments signal to your teen that their life and feelings are important to you, regardless of the busyness of life.

They provide a regular touchpoint that can help you catch early signs of issues or changes in your teen's mood or behavior, as well as offer timely support or intervention.

Exercise: Communication Role-Play

Get ready to step into each other's shoes and flex those communication muscles! We're turning your living room into a stage for the great parent-teen dialogue. It's like improv comedy, but with less laughs and more "I statements." We'll tackle scenarios ranging from the dreaded "bad grade discussion" to the classic "but all my friends have a later curfew" debate. You'll get to experience life on both sides of the parental divide, potentially discovering that being a teen isn't all TikTok dances and memes, and being a parent isn't just about saying "because I said so." It's a chance to practice open-ended questions, active listening, and creating a judgment-free zone, all while potentially uncovering your hidden talent for diplomatic negotiations. So, clear your throat, put on your best active listening face, and let's dive into some role-play that might just revolutionize your family's communication game.

Objective

To improve family communication skills and build empathy through role-playing exercises.

Materials

- List of scenario ideas
- Timer (optional)
- Notepad for observations (optional)

Instructions

1. Choose a scenario from the list or create your own. Some ideas include:

- Discussing a poor grade
- Negotiating a later curfew
- Addressing a disagreement with a friend
- Talking about college or career plans
- Discussing social media usage

2. Decide who will play the parent and who will play the teen for the first round.

3. Set the scene and begin the role-play. Try to stay in character for 5-10 minutes.

4. During the role-play, focus on:

- Using open-ended questions
- Practicing active listening
- Creating a safe, non-judgmental space for dialogue
- Expressing emotions clearly and respectfully

5. After the role-play, take a few minutes to discuss:

- What felt comfortable or uncomfortable?
- What techniques worked well?
- What would you do differently next time?
- How did it feel to be in the other person's position?

6. Switch roles and choose a new scenario for another round.

7. After a few rounds, reflect as a family:

- What did you learn about each other's perspectives?
- How can you apply these skills in real-life conversations?
- What areas of communication do you want to improve as a family?

This exercise can help both parents and teens develop better communication skills, build empathy for each other's perspectives, and create a foundation for more open and effective dialogues in the future. Plus, you might discover your family has a knack for improvisational theater – future family talent show, anyone?

Setting Healthy Boundaries: Online and Offline

In a digital landscape that evolves at an ever-rapid pace, guiding your teen to navigate their online and offline lives safely and responsibly requires a delicate balance. It's about setting limits and protection while also fostering a sense of moral responsibility and independence.

Discussing internet safety is as much about protecting your teen from external threats as it is about educating them on the responsibilities that come with digital freedoms. Initiating open discussions about the risks of online activity lays the groundwork for a safer digital environment. It's crucial to discuss common pitfalls such as oversharing personal information, engaging with strangers, and encountering inappropriate content. Providing clear, age-appropriate guidelines helps teens understand what safe online behavior looks like. For example, discussing the implications of sharing personal details and the permanence of online posts can encourage more thoughtful interactions with digital content.

Balancing the freedom teens crave with the oversight necessary for their safety is challenging but crucial. As teens push for more independence, it's important to gradually expand their freedoms while maintaining a safety net. To strike this balance, establish boundaries that gradually broaden as your teen demonstrates maturity and understanding of safe practices. For instance, you might start with strict limits on social media time, which could be relaxed as your teen shows they can handle the responsibility without it affecting their other obligations or emotional well-being.

The issue of privacy versus monitoring is particularly thorny for many families. While it's important to respect your teen's need for private conversations and space, both online and offline, it's equally important to ensure their activities are safe and appropriate. Finding a balance often comes down to open communication about the level of monitoring you believe is necessary, why it's needed, and how it will be conducted. Rather than covert surveillance, opt for a transparent approach where your teen is aware of the monitoring and the reasons for it. This could mean having access to their social media accounts but respecting their space by not commenting on every post or conversation they're part of unless there's a safety concern. This transparency helps build trust and understanding, demonstrating that your primary concern is their safety rather than controlling their social interactions.

Negotiating rules together can be one of the most effective ways to ensure that boundaries are respected. When teens are involved in drawing their own lines, they're more likely to adhere to them. This process should be collaborative, allowing both parents and teens an opportunity to express their concerns and preferences. For example, you and your teen could work together to create a 'digital curfew' — a time at night after which all devices are put away. Additionally, discussing and setting rules about meeting online friends in person can be crucial for safety. These conversations should emphasize mutual respect for each other's viewpoints and a shared commitment to safety.

Encouraging Independence While Offering Support

Fostering decision-making skills is essential because it directly impacts their ability to handle challenges, opportunities, and make the day-to-day choices that shape their lives. Facilitate this growth by involving your teen in everyday decisions that affect them, from choosing weekly meal plans to deciding which extracurricular activities to join. This inclusion not only makes them feel valued but also enhances their ability to weigh options and anticipate outcomes.

When discussing bigger decisions, such as high school courses or summer jobs, guide them through a structured decision-making process. This can involve identifying goals, gathering information, considering potential outcomes, and evaluating alternatives. For example, if your teen is deciding which subjects to choose, discuss their long-term goals, research the subjects' requirements and implications for future college applications, and consider their interests and aptitude in each subject. Encourage them to list pros and cons, and allow them the space to make the final decision. It's also important to discuss the benefits of making choices that don't turn out as planned. Emphasize that each decision is a learning opportunity, opening up the possibility that 'mistakes' are often just steps toward greater wisdom.

Supporting without solving is a delicate balance. As your teen inevitably faces challenges they need to learn to handle independently, your instinct to protect and solve problems can be strong. Resisting this urge and instead supporting them in finding their own solutions is key to fostering their problem-solving skills and resilience. Start by being a good listener when your teen shares a problem, fighting the temptation to offer solutions immediately. Instead, ask guiding questions that encourage them to think critically and explore potential options. For instance, if they're dealing with a conflict with a friend, rather than suggesting what they should do, ask, "What do you think might help resolve this situation?" or "What outcome are you hoping for from this conflict?"

Encouraging exploration of interests is vital during the teenage years. One of the joys of adolescence is the discovery of new passions that can influence career choices and lifelong hobbies. Encourage your teen to explore various interests by providing opportunities to try new activities. This could mean enrolling them in diverse classes, from art to coding, or encouraging participation in various clubs and sports. Maintain an open dialogue about what they enjoy or dislike about each activity, helping them to reflect on and understand their preferences.

Teaching financial independence is a critical life skill that promotes independence and responsibility. Begin by discussing budgeting basics. Help them create their own budget, perhaps starting with managing their allowance or earnings from part-time work. Teach them to track their income and expenses, set saving goals, and make informed spending decisions. Budgeting apps and spreadsheets can make this process more engaging and tangible. Involve your teen in age-appropriate family financial discussions. Explain the reasoning behind how you budget for family expenses, savings, and investments, as well as the financial considerations for family decisions like vacations or major purchases. This openness demystifies financial management and prepares them for their financial responsibilities in adulthood.

Exercise: Personal Interest Project

Whether your teen has always dreamed of writing the next great American novel, coding an app that'll make Mark Zuckerberg jealous, or starting a dog-walking empire, now's their time to shine. Think of it as their own personal Shark Tank, minus the intimidating billionaires and with 100% more supportive parents. Grab your thinking caps, dust off those ideas you've been hiding, and let's turn your family's passion into a project that you'll all be excited about

Objective

To encourage independence, foster creativity, and develop project management skills through the planning and execution of a personal interest project.

Materials

- Notebook or digital document for project planning
- Calendar for timeline creation
- Resources related to the chosen project (books, online tutorials, supplies, etc.)
- Vision board materials (optional)

Instructions

1. Brainstorm and Choose:

- Have your teen list their interests, hobbies, and dream projects
- Discuss the feasibility of each idea
- Choose one project to focus on (e.g., creating a short film, learning a new language, starting a small business)

2. Set Goals and Create a Timeline:

- Help your teen define clear, achievable goals for their project
- Break the project into smaller, manageable tasks
- Create a timeline for completing each task
- Consider using a visual aid like a Gantt chart or a simple calendar

3. Plan and Gather Resources:

- Encourage your teen to research what they'll need for the project
- Help them identify and acquire necessary resources
- Discuss potential challenges and brainstorm solutions

4. Execute and Monitor:

- Let your teen take the lead in project execution
- Schedule regular check-ins (weekly or bi-weekly) to discuss progress
- During check-ins, ask open-ended questions like:

  - What's been the most exciting part so far?
  - What challenges have you faced, and how did you overcome them?
  - What's your next step?

5. Provide Support:

- Offer guidance when asked, but resist the urge to take over
- Help your teen problem-solve when they hit roadblocks
- Provide encouragement and acknowledge their efforts

6. Reflect and Celebrate:

- Upon completion, have a "Project Showcase" where your teen presents their work
- Discuss what they learned about the subject and about themselves
- Celebrate their effort, creativity, and perseverance, regardless of the outcome
- Consider how this project might influence future goals or interests

Remember, the goal isn't perfection – it's growth, learning, and building confidence. This project is a chance for your teen to explore their interests, develop valuable skills, and maybe even discover a life-long passion. Who knows? This could be the start of the next big thing, or at least a really cool story for future job interviews!

Celebrating Progress: Acknowledging Efforts and Achievements

Celebrating progress and acknowledging efforts and achievements is crucial in the intricate dance of raising teens. It's about recognizing the small victories and incremental advancements that often go unnoticed in the daily hustle. Celebrating these moments can significantly impact your teen's motivation and self-esteem, turning even the smallest triumphs into springboards for future accomplishments. As parents, fostering an environment where every effort is acknowledged not only builds a supportive atmosphere but also instills a sense of accomplishment and pride in your teenager.

Recognizing small victories is essential because it reinforces the positive behaviors and efforts that lead to these achievements. For instance, if your teen has been struggling with math and their grade improves even slightly, it's a moment worth celebrating. This doesn't require grand gestures; sometimes, acknowledgment can be as simple as a congratulatory note on the refrigerator or a special mention at dinner. These affirmations make the effort tangible, showing your teen that their hard work isn't going unnoticed. It's about validating their journey and making the connection between perseverance and results clear and rewarding. Regularly celebrating these small victories keeps motivation alive, especially in areas where your child may not naturally excel but is putting in the effort to improve.

Creating a culture of praise within the family involves more than occasional compliments; it requires a consistent approach to recognizing and appreciating effort, regardless of the outcome. This can be achieved by taking time to reflect on each family member's contributions and achievements, perhaps during weekly family meetings or casual conversations. Discuss not just what was accomplished, but how it was accomplished, emphasizing the creativity, perseverance, or courage involved. This practice helps shift the focus from outcome-based recognition to effort-based praise, which is crucial in fostering resilience and a growth mindset. When teens realize that their efforts are valued regardless of the result, they are more likely to take on challenges and persist in the face of difficulties.

Using encouragement as motivation is closely tied to how praise is articulated. Positive reinforcement, when used effectively, can boost a teen's willingness to keep pushing through challenges. It's about catching them in the act of figuring things out and reinforcing that behavior with positive feedback that is specific and timely. For example, if you notice your teen is making an effort to keep their room organized, a specific compliment like, "I really appreciate how you've kept your room tidy this week; it makes the whole house feel nicer," can be more motivating than a generic "good job." This specificity not only makes the praise more genuine but also directs your teen to the behaviors that are valued and expected. Additionally, coupling praise with tangible rewards that align with your family values—like extra privileges or choice-based incentives—can motivate teens to maintain their positive behaviors.

Reflecting on growth regularly is another crucial component of celebrating progress. This involves looking back over time to recognize the developments and changes that have occurred. It can be facilitated through family discussions, where each member shares their personal growth highlights and challenges, or through private journals that record thoughts and experiences over time. These reflections allow teens to see for themselves how far they've come, making the abstract concept of growth more concrete and recognizable. They provide a sense of progression that can be incredibly satisfying and motivating. Moreover, these reflections offer valuable insights into the areas where they still need support, allowing you as a parent to better understand how you can aid their ongoing development.

Resources for Further Support: Where to Turn When You Need Help

Navigating adolescence is a complex process filled with unique challenges and milestones. While parents and caregivers provide a primary layer of support, there are times when professional assistance becomes necessary to ensure a teenager's well-being. Understanding when and how to seek this help is crucial.

Identifying when professional help is needed is the first step in ensuring your teen's well-being. Look for signs that might indicate a need for professional intervention. These signs can vary widely, ranging from persistent feelings of sadness or anxiety that disrupt daily activities to noticeable changes in behavior such as withdrawal from social connections, drastic changes in eating or sleeping patterns, or unexplained declines in academic performance.

Finding the right resources is essential when such signs emerge. It's important to take action by seeking out professionals who specialize in adolescent issues. Finding the right therapist or counselor can feel overwhelming, but it starts with a few key steps. You might begin by consulting your family doctor, who can provide a referral, or by using trusted resources like the American Psychological Association's psychologist locator. When choosing a therapist, it's important to consider their specialization in teen treatment and approach to therapy, ensuring it aligns with your teen's needs and your family's values. Additionally, involving your teen in the selection process can empower them and enhance their comfort level with the treatment process.

Utilizing school resources can often serve as valuable support systems and provide immediate assistance. Most schools have trained guidance counselors who understand the intricacies of adolescent life and are equipped to provide short-term counseling, crisis intervention, and referrals to longer-term support if necessary. Additionally, many schools have peer support programs and other initiatives designed to promote mental well-being among students. Familiarizing yourself and your teen with these resources can provide them with additional layers of support that are readily accessible in their daily environment.

Online and community resources offer a wealth of tools that can be valuable in supporting teenagers and parents. Websites like Teen Mental Health or Young Minds offer a plethora of information, including articles, toolkits, and contact information for crisis services. Online forums and support groups can also offer anonymity and accessibility, providing both teens and parents with a platform to share experiences and solutions in a supportive setting. However, it's crucial to vet these online resources carefully to ensure they are reputable and provide accurate, helpful information.

As you incorporate these resources into your support strategy, remember that every teen's needs are unique. What works for one may not work for another, and sometimes finding the right support can take time. The key is persistence and open communication, ensuring your teen feels supported and heard throughout the process. By utilizing a combination of personal support, professional help, and educational resources, you can create a comprehensive support system that empowers your teen to navigate the challenges of adolescence with greater resilience and confidence.

A Chance to Pay It Forward

As you turn the last pages of this book, please take a moment to hold the door open for someone else – for another parent that may be experiencing similar challenges with their teen.

Simply by sharing one to two sentences about your own journey with your teen, you'll show new readers where they can find all the guidance they need to enhance their teens' social skills too.

Please scan the QR code to leave a review.

Thank you so much for your support. We're all on our own parenting journeys, but every ounce of help we can share makes a huge impact to our future generation.

Conclusion

We've made it! From decoding the impact of smartphones on socializing to navigating the treacherous waters of social anxiety, we've covered it all. We've explored how to build those crucial social skills, the ones that'll help your teen navigate life without constantly feeling like they're starring in their own personal awkward sitcom.

Remember when we talked about communication, empathy, emotional regulation, resilience, conflict resolution, active listening, and self-esteem? Those aren't just fancy words to impress at dinner parties. These are the superpowers your teen needs to conquer their social world. Think of them as the Avengers of social skills, each one powerful on its own, but unstoppable when combined.

Now, let's talk about those exercises throughout the book. They're not just there to fill space or give you an excuse to spend more time with your teen (although that's a nice bonus). These activities are your secret weapon in understanding and bonding with your teen. They're like a cheat code for parenting, but without the guilt of actually cheating.

This book isn't just about giving you a bunch of information to file away in your "I'll get to it someday" folder. It's about empowering you to be the superhero sidekick in your teen's journey. We're equipping you with the knowledge and strategies to support your teen's social development effectively. Think of yourself as the Alfred to their Batman, the Q to their James Bond, the... well, you get the idea.

But here's the thing, the social landscape is always changing. What's cool today might be cringe-worthy tomorrow. (Just ask anyone who still says "groovy".) That's why it's crucial to stay open, adaptable, and proactive. Keep learning, keep adjusting, and for the love of all that is holy, please try to understand what TikTok is.

Now, here's your call to action: Don't just read this book and put it on a shelf to gather dust. Use it! Engage with the activities, try out the strategies, create that supportive environment. Your teen's future self will thank you (even if their current self rolls their eyes at you).

Remember, you've got this! With the right tools and mindset, you can help your teen navigate the complexities of social interactions with the grace of a... well, maybe not a swan, but at least a slightly clumsy duckling. And that's progress!

If you're feeling overwhelmed (and let's face it, who isn't?), don't worry. There are plenty of resources out there to help you on this journey. Check out online forums, community programs, or professional services. It takes a village to raise a child, and in the digital age, that village might just be a Facebook group.

Before we wrap this up, I want to get a little personal. As someone who's passionate about helping parents and teens navigate the social challenges of the digital age, I want to thank you. Thank you for caring enough to read this book, for wanting to understand and support your teen, and for embarking on this important journey. Your dedication to improving your teen's life is truly inspiring.

So, let's keep this conversation going. Let's work together to build a future where our teens can confidently and empathetically engage with the world around them. Because at the end of the day, that's what it's all about - raising kids who aren't just socially savvy, but kind, empathetic, and ready to take on the world.

Here's to you, to your teens, and to a future filled with meaningful connections and fewer awkward silences.

With gratitude and a shared eye roll at dad jokes,

Amber Preston

References

Cavaness, K., Picchioni, A., & Fleshman, J. W. (2020). Linking Emotional Intelligence to Successful Health Care Leadership: The Big Five Model of Personality. *Clinics in Colon and Rectal Surgery, 33*(04), 195–203. NCBI. https://doi.org/10.1055/s-0040-1709435

Dweck, C. (2012). *Mindset: How You Can Fulfill Your Potential.* Robinson.

Leigh, E., & Clark, D. M. (2018). Understanding Social Anxiety Disorder in Adolescents and Improving Treatment Outcomes: Applying the Cognitive Model of Clark and Wells (1995). *Clinical Child and Family Psychology Review, 21*(3), 388–414. https://doi.org/10.1007/s10567-018-0258-5

www.ingramcontent.com/pod-product-compliance
Lightning Source LLC
Chambersburg PA
CBHW071708120626
46550CB00001B/148